THE FIRST WORLD WAR

EPHEMERA MEMENTOES DOCUMENTS

THE FIRST WORLD WAR

ephemera
mementoes
documents

MAURICE RICKARDS MICHAEL MOODY

JUPITER BOOKS 1975

Jupiter Books (London) Limited
167 Hermitage Road London N4

SBN 904041 212

Filmset, printed and bound by
R. J. Acford Ltd., Industrial Estate,
Chichester, Sussex

First published 1975

INTRODUCTION

This book owes its origins to an exhibition presented in the summer of 1970 at the Imperial War Museum, London. Devised and arranged by Michael Moody, and appearing under the title 'Ephemera of The First World War', the exhibition collected together for the first time the war's printed marginalia – the oddments and mementoes of day-to-day life of a world in conflict.

The field had till that time been more or less neglected; war posters had had major showings in books and exhibitions all over the world, but the unconsidered trifles of charity flags, souvenirs and other such items had remained for the most part parenthetic–unorganized, uncatalogued and largely unpublished. The exhibition gave formal recognition to the status of this material as a medium of social-history record.

The present collection takes for its nucleus items appearing in the exhibition and adds further material derived from subsequent research in the museum and elsewhere. Thanks are due to the trustees and directors of the Imperial War Museum for their cooperation in allowing exhibits to be photographed, and to a number of private collectors who have kindly lent material for inclusion.

In addition to specimens from private and public collections, some are included which have found their way to these pages by less formal means. The saleroom, the secondhand shop, and occasionally the street barrow, have all yielded exhibits. To the unknown original owners of these items, or to their successors, the compilers convey their acknowledgements and thanks.

If some of the items appear in less than pristine condition, they are no less valid for that. On the contrary, to the collector of ephemera, as well as to the social historian, the creased and dog-eared item from yesterday's pocketbook is as redolent of its time as any in mint condition – often more so. The reader will also bear in mind that, with many of these items, the wonder is that they have survived at all.

A word as to captions. Place-names indicate place of publication, not necessarily the nationality of the publisher. Thus, for example, although item No 6 is of German origin, its place of publication is Belgium; Belgium therefore is named in the caption. The principle may at first sight appear misleading, but designation by the more obvious method would unfortunately be more so. A proclamation issued by the British Army in France could not reasonably carry the foot-line *Britain*. Nor, similarly, could a postcard from a British PoW camp in Upper Silesia. Interpenetration of nationality is inherent in the context; any anomaly of captioning must be taken as a reflection of the anomaly of war.

ACKNOWLEDGEMENTS

The authors and publishers acknowledge with thanks the help, advice and cooperation of the director and staff of the Imperial War Museum, London. As indicated in the preface, the book derives directly from an exhibition of a selection of the Museum's collection of war ephemera held in 1970. More than half of the items reproduced here are Museum exhibits, and library and other facilities provided by the Museum have contributed much in the preparation of the text.

Special thanks are due to Mr Joseph Darracott, Keeper of the Museum's Department of Art, for permission to photograph and reproduce exhibits and for the granting of special research facilities.

Among members of the Museum staff who have contributed valuable help and advice, mention must be made of Miss Diana Condell, Miss Rose Coombes, Miss Rosemary Hands, Dr D G Baylis, and Mr James Lucas.

The authors and publishers are particularly indebted to Mr V Rigby, also of the Museum staff, whose encyclopedic knowledge and research acumen has been invaluable. The book owes much to his help and guidance.

Thanks are also due to a number of other institutions and individuals. The help of the staff of the Victoria and Albert Museum is gratefully acknowledged, as well as that of the Trustees of the British Museum and the Director of the Fitzroy Collection. Among private individuals who have helped with research, information or the loan of exhibits, thanks are due to Mr Henry Bristow, Mr Merwin Dembling, Mr Hans Freytag, Mrs Johanna Harrison, Mr Peter Jackson, Miss Yolanda Martelli, Mr Peter Opie, Miss Kay Robertson, Mr Patrick Robertson and Mr Peter T Scott.

The authors also extend their thanks to Mr David Lambert for services in colour photography and to PEN Photographics Ltd for special facilities in the preparation of originals for reproduction.

THE FIRST WORLD WAR

Ephemera, Mementoes and Documents

Today, as the century looks toward its end, Pandora's box is still only partly open: the worst may be yet to come. But it was in August 1914, barely a year or two from turn-of-the-century innocence, that mankind first prised up the lid. The First World War was an event without precedent. Previous wars had killed their tens of thousands; this one was to kill its millions.

By the end of that August week, when the last dispositions and the formal declarations of war had been made, to many it still seemed to be a war like any other. A biggish war, perhaps, with an uncommonly large number of contestants, but an orthodox up-and-at-'em war 'over by Christmas', as they said in London; 'before the leaves fall', as they said in Berlin.

But by Christmas there were tens of thousands of dead, with nothing but immobility to show for the cost. Millions of men, bogged down in an unbroken front from the sea to the alps, faced each other across a shattered landscape. It began to look as though something had gone wrong.

It was to stay that way for nearly four years. The battle line, while it devoured men and materials on a scale unmatched in history, moved back and forth over the same ground within a range of only a few miles, almost to the end.

By 1918, casualty figures had reached proportions that governments on all sides were loath to dwell upon. Even today the official total is conjecture. Give or take a few hundred thousand, the final count was eight and a half million dead. Total casualties, including wounded and missing, were reckoned at over thirty millions. It was in no sense a war like any other. Ultimately everyone came to recognize how different it was.

Not least among its novelties was the impact of mass production. New technologies and distribution methods had changed the face of nineteenth-century industry. Everywhere, as ever after in this century, statistics soared. When war came, the new techniques took over: production rates, now in the service of destruction, redoubled. The age of the multiple product demanded the multiple weapon, the multiple shell – and soon the multiple man.

It was also the age of the multiple message. The art of printing, itself the archetype of mass production, became a weapon of war as relevant as the making of munitions. Proliferation of word and image was as predictable a mass-production statistic as all the rest: how else could the flame of war be fanned, how else its organization and methods controlled?

On a scale that had only been guessed at before, the multiple message burgeoned. In encouragement and cajolement, coercion and control, in a score of languages and dialects, the printed image multiplied. On all sides the presses poured forth war.

There was the hard stuff: enlistment orders, ration books, forms, message-pads, official notices and proclamations; there was the middling range of government posters, leaflets and brochures – exhortative, instructive and minatory – and there was the soft periphery of commerical and other enterprise; books, magazines, newspapers, charity flags, souvenirs, advertisements, labels, postcards. Here was the whole gamut of war on paper, public private, personal – and, to printers at least, profitable.

It was an explosion as spectacular, and in its own way as significant, as the rest of the mass-production scene. And like the other products of the period, like the solid-tyred ambulances and the spike-topped German helmets, these items are true reflections of their age. In their visual style, their layout, subject matter and terminology, they speak often explicitly, often in detailed chapter and verse. Only in a corset advertisement [23]* and only in early August 1914, could the advertiser's view of war appear so graphically; only in a war decree for the suspension of Sunday as a day of rest [4] could the German view of imperial discipline be expressed with such economy and bite.

But as well as providing detail, these oddments convey a general view. We see not only cupidity and special pleading, but the broad sweep of mood and morale as the war progresses. The chronology is clear: there is initially the sudden upward curve of optimism, then briefly the heights of soaring certainty, and soon the long tired decline as year follows year and reality takes over. The Great War story starts in a golden haze and finishes in exhaustion and dismay. Collectively, the nations see their nineteenth-century image fade: the flagwaving, the ceremonial, the chivalry, the old heraldics, pass. Within a few months naivety has vanished. What is left is nasty, brutish and long.

It is in its initial naivety that the picture is most striking. The mementoes, ephemera and documents of early 1914 have an awful simplicity. They convey only the most grotesquely inadequate estimate of the nature of things to come and only the most superficial grasp of what was already going on. It was a state of affairs which, at some levels, in spite of subsequent disenchantment, was to prevail throughout the war. The soldier on leave from the trenches, abstracted from his familiar scene of death and disaster, was soon to observe the dichotomy; as things got worse the people at home had a less and less distinct idea of the truth. It became impossible to tell them. Ultimately the man from the trenches gave up trying.

With twentieth-century hindsight the naivety of 1914 appears incredible. Could people really think that this was just another foreign skirmish, another Boer War, another little local difficulty?

It must be said at once that the universal lack of prescience was not confined to those left at home. Among the generals too there survived attitudes from the eighteen hundreds – and earlier. Still the view was widely held that war was an affair of battlefields, hollow squares and cavalry charges, a set-piece engagement for professionals. A conservative attitude was the hallmark of Europe's military caste on both sides of the channel. By background and breeding the soldier-leader was the natural opponent of change. The routines and maxims of the battlefield, like those of his private life, were as inviolate as the laws of nature. It was thus that generals everywhere acquired a reputation for fighting each new war with the handbooks of the last. Thus, that the poilu of 1914 went into action in the blue tunic and bright red trousers of the 1870s; thus that the British soldier, fresh from Empire over palm and pine, did duty throughout the war in tropical puttees.

Resistance to change was all-pervading. It touched matters great and small. Among the minor hazards of trench warfare was the reflectivity of uniform buttons; their metallic gleam provided useful points of focus for the aim of snipers; soon it became apparent that dull buttons would be more suitable. But it was a long time before anything was done about it. In November 1914 a French soldier wrote to a friend, 'I must again bother you for assistance. You probably know that we are obliged to darken

* Figures in brackets refer to illustrations.

our brass buttons. The means at our disposal are necessarily primitive. What happens is that mine, for example, which were darkened in a bath of lead acetate, are now regaining their former brilliance. Would you know of a *bronzing* method perhaps – a simple one, and which would *last*? I thank you in advance. You can imagine what a business it is, the continual unsewing and resewing of them . . .'

The steel helmet, which was later to become almost a symbol of World War I, itself took a long time to materialize. Apart from the sabre-proof *Pickelhaube* of the Germans, the soft hat was universal among the soldiery of 1914. Only slowly was it conceded that the weapons of the twentieth century called for something more substantial.

Statistical analysis began to reveal that a high percentage of fatalities in battle were due to head wounds. It appeared that a protective helmet of some kind might obviate a number of these.

The 'new steel helmets', latest in new-fangled innovations, began to appear toward the end of 1915. So new and unexpected were they that press pictures of helmeted troops continued to carry explanatory notes ('The troops are wearing the new steel headgear') throughout 1916 and into 1917.

The German 'spikeless' helmet appeared just one year after the declaration of war. When an advance guard of Americans arrived in Europe in 1917 (wearing soft hats), they were at first given French steel helmets, then British ones. As late as May 1918, one magazine showing a Belgian vizored helmet thought it worth commenting that steel helmets were 'now worn by all the combatants'.

At the operational end of the scale, we have the British Army's version of the Cavalry Charge [42]: 'On the command "charge" one cheer will be given, the front rank will bring swords to the swords in line and every man will tighten his grip of the saddle and increase his speed with the fixed determination of riding the enemy down . . .' Trench warfare, it must be admitted, had not been fully envisaged.

But no assessment of the naiveties of 1914 can be valid without reference to the wider context. What kind of world was it that went to war that summer? What was its social and economic climate, the level of its technology, the state of its moral development?

It was a late Victorian world. Though squarely set in the twentieth-century scene, though lapped by novelty, by the motor car, the flying machine and the tango, it was a world still not wholly disentangled from the eighteen fifties.

There had been a relaxing sigh at the turn of the century. In Britain the Old Queen and her world had finally gone. The new world breathed a little easier. But the effect of two or three generations of Victorian stability were slow to fade. The early nineteen hundreds, for all their heavier-than-air machines and moving pictures, still bore signs of their parentage.

As the lamps began to go out all over Europe there were millions for whom only yesterday it had been a world of Oscar Wilde, Nietzsche, Whistler, Chekhov, Toulouse-Lautrec, Ruskin, Gauguin . . . Only a year or two ago Florence Nightingale had still been alive. There were people for whom the Great Exhibition was a living memory, people who had met Charles Dickens, who had actually been to the Duke of Wellington's funeral, who remembered the American Civil War and the death of Abraham Lincoln.

1914 was the year John Tenniel died. He could remember the time of George Stephenson's *Rocket*, of Michael Faraday and William Hazlitt and the Tolpuddle Martyrs. There was Lord Roberts, hero of South Africa: he could remember the repeal of the Corn Laws. And Horatio Herbert Kitchener: he could remember the first telephone, and the first telegraphed despatches from the Crimea.

There was the Emperor of Germany, Class of 1859; Franz-Joseph, 1830; King George V, 1865 – all reliably nineteenth-century men. For all of these, and for most of the population, old values and old attitudes clung on.

Poverty clung on too. In 1914 the average wage of the British working man was £1 a week. Up to a half of that might go on rent. A second-hand pair of boots might cost five shillings (25p). Average weekly expenditure for a manual worker's family was ten shillings (50p). There was not much room for extravagance.

Hand-in-hand with poverty went squalor and ill-health. Overcrowding, bad sanitation, disease and a high death-rate were the commonly accepted facts of workingclass life. Conditions had changed little through the previous century. Cholera was less a threat. So was typhus. But for the rest, the products of squalor and overcrowding went largely unchallenged. Dr Barnardo's pictorial rendering [168] was only slightly over-drawn.

Infant mortality rates were scarcely changed from the levels of 1800. In the London parish of St George's-in-the-East in 1900, out of a total of 1259 deaths, 661 were of children under five years of age. Hospitals were supported by charity; doctors were supported by fees. There was no Health Service; sickness and unemployment insurance were experimental novelties. The pill-pedlar, the market-place quack and the cure-all industry flourished. So did the moneylender, the palm reader and the abortionist.

Privilege clung on too. The rich man and the poor man remained where the hymn-book had respectively placed them. The Royal Family, not yet fully free of the suspicion of Divine Right, ruled over its loving subject peoples. It was not for nothing that His Majesty, in August 1914, was able to use the personal possessive in his message to the troops as they left for France [3]: 'You are leaving home to fight for the safety and honour of my Empire . . .' In that same August the Kaiser spoke in similar terms: 'You, my troops, are my guarantee that I can dictate peace to my enemies . . .'

Nor was it for nothing that the various monarchs (or whoever wrote their speeches) invoked the help of God: 'I pray God to bless you and guard you and bring you back victorious,' said George V to his troops as they left to fight for his empire. 'I trust implicity in the help of God,' said Wilhelm II, as he moved from Berlin to a safer part of the country. These monarchs' affinity, both with the deity and the Victorian era, was unchallengeable. They shared not only the same God and the same style in proclamations but, in Victoria herself, the same grandmother.

It is to be noted, in the matter of proclamations, that here too conservatism ruled. As with the military, the old methods – even the old phraseology – served best. When George V put on a food economy appeal in 1917 he did so in a form almost indistinguishable from a proclamation of his predecessor on a similar occasion a hundred and fourteen years earlier*:

1917. By the King: A PROCLAMATION. *George R.I.* We being persuaded that the abstention from all unnecessary consumption of grain will furnish the surest and most effectual means of defeating the devices of our enemies and thereby of bringing the war to a successful and speedy termination, and out of our resolve to leave nothing undone which can contribute to those ends

---

* 1800: By the King: A PROCLAMATION. *George R.* Whereas an address has been presented to us by our two Houses of Parliament requesting us to issue our Royal Proclamation recommending to all such persons as have the means of procuring other articles of food the greatest economy and frugality in the use of every species of grain: We having taken the said Address into consideration and being persuaded that the prevention of all unnecessary consumption of corn will furnish one of the surest and most effectual means of alleviating the present pressure and of providing for the necessary demands of the year, have therefore in pursuance of the said Address and out of our tender concern for the welfare of our people thought fit (with the advice of our Privy Council) to issue this our Royal Proclamation, most earnestly exhorting and charging all those of our loving subjects who have the means of procuring other articles of food than corn, as they tender their own immediate interests and feel for the wants of others, to practise the greatest

or to the welfare of our people in these times of grave stress and anxiety, have thought fit by and with the advice of our Privy Council to issue this our Royal Proclamation most earnestly exhorting and charging all those of our loving subjects the men and women of our realm who have the means of procuring articles of food other than wheaten corn, as they tender their own immediate interest and feel for the want of others, especially to practise the greatest economy and frugality in the use of every species of grain: And we do for this purpose more particularly exhort and charge all the heads of households to reduce consumption of bread in their respective families by at least one fourth of the quantity consumed in ordinary times, to abstain from the use of flour in pastry, and moreover carefully to restrict or wherever possible to abandon the use thereof in all other articles than bread. And we do also in like manner exhort and charge all persons who keep horses to abandon the practice of feeding the same on oats or other grain unless they shall have received from our Food Controller a licence to feed horses on oats or other grain to be given only in cases where it is necessary to do so with a view to maintain the breed of horses in the national interest. And we do hereby further charge and enjoin all ministers of religion in their respective churches and chapels within our United Kingdom of Great Britain and Ireland to read or cause to be read this our Proclamation on the Lord's Day for four successive weeks after the issue thereof. Given at our Court at Buckingham Palace this second day of May in the year of Our Lord one thousand and seventeen in the seventh year of our reign. God Save the King.

Apart from a change of address, the nationality of the foe, and other details, history appears to have stood still.

It did so for the Upper Classes too. It was still possible in 1914 for newspaper small ad sections to carry long columns headed *Horses and Carriages*. There were also listings under *Housemaids, Parlourmaids, Between-Maids, Kitchen-Maids* and *Domestics*. Butlers, valets and footmen still offered their services. *The Times* had Lady Experts who advised the gentry on the syntax of their staff advertisements. The newspaper ventured to mention the fact; under the heading *Mistresses Seeking Good Servants* it permitted itself to quote satisfied clients: 'I got a Between-maid from my last advertisement and had several other answers. I find, too that one gets a much better class of servant applying than those one meets in registry offices'. Readers were apparently unanimous on the quality aspect: 'Mrs Strange has always found *The Times* an excellent paper to advertise in for domestic servants, and as a result has always been able to engage quite a superior class of girl . . .'

A seigneurial attitude to employees survived even into the later years of the war, when 'the servant problem' had become a standard middle-class talking point. It appeared also in industry and the public utilities, where the army recruitment authorities wrangled with civilian employers for the services of men for the trenches [32]. Under the heading 'The War' one display advertisement searched the industrialist conscience: 'Have you seen to it that every fit man under your control has been given the opportunity of enlisting?' After further and more detailed questioning the potential purveyor of recruits is reminded of the moral virtue of his sacrifice: 'Your country will appreciate the help you give. More men are wanted TODAY. What can you do?'

---

economy and frugality in the use of every species of grain: And we do for this purpose more particularly exhort and charge all masters of families to reduce the consumption of bread in their respective families by at least one third of the quantity consumed in ordinary times, and in no case to suffer the same to exceed one quartern loaf for each person in each week, to abstain from the use of flour in pastry, and moreover carefully to restrict the use thereof in all other articles than bread: And we do also in like manner exhort and charge all persons who keep horses, especially horses for pleasure, as far as their respective circumstances will admit carefully to restrict the consumption of oats and other grain for the subsistence of the same. And we do hereby further charge and command every minister in his respective parish church or chapel within the Kingdom of Great Britain to read or cause to be read our said Proclamation. Given at our Court of St. James's the third day of December one thousand eight hundred in the forty-first year of our reign. God Save the King.

A month or two later the spotlight turns on the stately home: '5 Questions to those who employ male servants' [9]. With its list of possible candidates — butler, groom, chauffeur, gardener or gamekeeper — it graphically evokes its period hunting ground. And with a stirring appeal to the gentleman of the house to sacrifice his personal convenience for his country's need, it neatly expresses a commodity view of manpower. It concludes, as, by genealogical descent from the royal proclamation, all such items concluded, with 'God Save the King'. It is possibly the last true vestige of the neo-baronial ever to appear in public print.

The British stately home, it must be remembered, though today familiar as a museum of social history, was in 1915 still a going concern. In spirit, at least, it was also a wartime export. When Lord Northcliffe visited Haig at his headquarters somewhere in France, he found the concept carrying on within the sound of gunfire. In his commandeered country house 'the life of Sir Douglas Haig might seem to be that of some great Scotch laird who chooses to direct his estates himself'. It may be wondered whether the troops on the Somme read this report. The same reporter, writing of Joffre at the height of the battle of Verdun assured his readers that 'today, in the midst of the colossal series of battles that has lasted for months, the head of the wonderful French war machine has the healthy look of a country squire in those good old days, two years ago, when men rode to hounds a couple of days a week'.

It must not be concluded that the upper classes stood aloof. They threw themselves, particularly their women, into war activity of all kinds. Often it was with a dedication amounting to frenzy. To some observers it seemed that there might be motives deeper than those of simple patriotism. Did the war, as for the lower orders, offer unhoped-for freedoms? Was this a case of emancipation from the top? Or was it partly an expiation of the guilt of being upper class? Whatever it was, it made good home-front copy. 'Emergency Cooking Classes in London', announced the 'Evening News', and continued, much diverted: 'The Society Woman is learning to cook . . . The mistress, for the first time in many cases, sees the inside of her own kitchen ...' It was good for morale.

A further survival from the pre-war world of the gentry was The Cure — the visit to a watering place. This too went on undaunted. 'The German Navy cannot navigate the Buxton waters', said the Buxton information office, 'Situate in the centre of England, Buxton is the *safest* and most restful place in the country.' Other resorts offered similar attractions: 'Don't worry about raids, but come to Cliftonville' [90]; 'Folkestone: Price of Provisions is Normal'. France too: 'Winter in Monte Carlo: Renowned thermal establishment: open all the year round'. And Germany: 'Wiesbaden: no interruption in the Wiesbaden Cure: Peaceful healthy stay: all hotels remain open.' For a while at least, all over Europe, for those who could manage to pay for it, history stood still.

Cavalry versus Machine Gun

Perhaps the most significant of surviving bygones was the horse. For their buses and cabs the capital of Europe had gone over fairly generally to petrol; trams were everywhere and urban electric railway stations dotted the major towns. But threading its way undisturbed through these new networks, the horse remained a universally accepted unit of conveyance. Each big city still had its quota of jobmasters, stables, ostlers, horse auctioneers and manure dealers. Contractors' carts, dust carts, milk delivery floats, brewers' drays, coal carts — these, the overwhelming majority of city vehicles, were still horse-drawn.

So were the vehicles of the armies. Virtually all military supplies were carried in horse-drawn trucks. Weapons, ammunition, food, medical supplies and the full panoply of war was moved, as it had been for centuries, by horses. For many millions of citizens the mounted gun-team and the cavalry brigade provided the complete epitome of martial might. When war came, mobilization entailed the mass requisition of horses [10, 11]. Taken from their shafts in the streets or delivered by appointment at designated centres, in every belligerent country horses joined the army in tens of thousands.

Notwithstanding the spectacular growth of railways and the motor car, it was substantially a horse-drawn war. One statistic records that of all the commodities shipped across the Channel by the British during the whole period 1914 – 1918, the greatest weight was in fodder. No small consideration was the cavalry. The military mind, apparently unmoved by the growth of war machines, could not bring itself to abandon the concept of the massed horseman.

The last successful cavalry charges had taken place at Waterloo. In the American Civil War, where the machine gun and trench warfare had first appeared, cavalrymen had adopted the role of mounted infantry, using their mounts largely for reconnaissance and limited raiding. But three years later, in the Austro-Prussian war of 1866, 56,000 cavalrymen, armed only with sabres and lances, charged into rifle- and gun-fire.

The 1870 war brought massed charges from both sides. Casualties were enormous. But the cavalry charge idea persisted. In the years immediately prior to 1914, regardless of machine guns, experts still advocated the horseman. One French expert wrote, in 1905: 'Thanks to their rapidity of movement, cavalry masses will play a preponderating role in future wars . . .' Experts in all countries agreed. Many of the leading generals of the day saw cavalry as a major arm – if only as the answer to the enemy's cavalry.

When General von Bernhardi's book on cavalry warfare appeared in English translation it met with widespread approval among the British. There was no mistaking the author's message: 'On the achievements of the cavalry in the early days of the war will depend to a considerable extent the success of the first great decisive encounter.' In a chapter on Independent Cavalry, von Bernhardi describes an attack: 'At the trumpet-call . . . the whole hurl themselves with the greatest determination and with loud cheers upon the enemy.'

The German general's book was admired by no less a person than Sir John French, commander of the British Expeditionary Force in France. Sir John went so far as to write a preface to the book, a special edition of which was published shortly after the war had started. In the preface he commended the writings of a British expert, Sir Evelyn Wood, who '. . . though seventy-two years of age is still one of the hardest and straightest riders to hounds in England'. But the Field-Marshal's main recommendation was the work of the German 'whose intimate knowledge of cavalry and brilliant writings have won for him such a great European reputation.' It was the duty of every cavalry officer, said French, 'to study profoundly the training, tactics and organisation of the best foreign cavalry' and to 'reflect long and deeply upon the opinions of such acknowledged authorities as Field-Marshal Sir Evelyn Wood and General von Bernhardi'. Sir John was relieved of his responsibilities on the Western Front at the end of 1915.

The role of the horse in war was deeply engraved in the public mind. No one thought it anything other than right and proper when the Kaiser declared: 'We shall resist to the last breath of man and horse.' In all of the war's imagery, in flag-day emblems, cigarette-cards, posters and postcards, the war-horse was a universal *leitmotiv*. In Germany, France, Austria, and particularly in Russia, cavalry-charge posters appeared in thousands. Typical, and even less than ordinarily credible, was the solo swordsman in Britain's 'Forward!' poster [76]. In magazines and newspaper illustrations, where sketches were produced often by men who had never left home, the cavalry melée and the galloping gun-team were favourite subjects. Northcliffe, in one of his 'despatches', writes from the mud of France: 'this war is a horrible, grim, mechanical business'. But he recalls wistfully: 'once on my way to the battle of Verdun, I came across something that looked like a war picture – a squadron of lancers with their pennants gaily streaming, preceded by a corps of buglers.' The image died hard.

Apart from Germany, where automatic weapons had been enthusiastically adopted, most countries deprecated the value of the machine gun. France's generals believed in all-out headlong attack – with two machine guns to a battalion. Even as late as 1915, by which time some million men had been killed by machine guns, cavalryman Sir Douglas Haig opined that two machine guns to a battalion was 'more than sufficient'.

Germany, in spite of her espousal of the machine gun, entered the war, like France, with ten cavalry divisions – some 70,000 men each. German Field Service Regulations [42] show that she saw them in the context of a machine-gun war. (A memorable item is paragraph 584: 'Machine guns, even when on their wheeled carriages, are able to emit a large volume of well-aimed fire in a short space of time.')

Britain too envisaged cavalry attacks, as her own Field Service Regulations indicate. On another page of the cavalry section she too allows of the presence of machine guns. Under the heading 'The Pursuit' appears the sentence: 'Guns and machine guns in a pursuit are most effective and must be used with great boldness'. But the main stress is on the melée, the classic climax of the cavalry charge: 'In a successful melée, determination, horsemanship and skilful use of the sword and lance decide the issue . . .' Earlier in the same section appears a passage in which Balaclava lives again:

In order to economise energy and retain cohesion for the shock, the attacking troops will remain for as long as possible at the trot: they will increase the pace to a gallop in sufficient time to permit of the charge being made with the necessary momentum, but cohesion must not be sacrificed for pace. Should an opportunity occur of surprising the enemy, or of striking him before or during deployment, the gallop may be commenced at a considerable distance from the objective . . . When the commander wishes to obtain the necessary momentum in anticipation of the charge (usually at about 300 to 500 yards distance from the enemy) he will give the command LINE WILL ATTACK. The pace will then be slightly increased, swords and lances will be brought to the engage, every horse must be thoroughly in hand, the men must be riding close, and there should be two distinct and well-defined ranks; troop leaders will be careful to keep their correct distance from the directing troop leader, and on no account should they exceed this distance; flank guides will press in towards the centre of their troops; the rear men will fill up any gaps which may occur in the rank in front of them . . . By his skill in choosing the right moment for the charge the leader can increase his chance of success. The shorter the distance over which the charge is made, the greater will be the cohesion and the fresher will be the horses for the actual shock. The charge should not be ordered, therefore, until the line is about 50 yards distant from the enemy . . . On the command CHARGE one cheer will be given, the front rank will bring swords to the swords in line, and every man will tighten his grip of the saddle and increase his speed with the fixed determination of riding the enemy down.

The concept of the cavalry charge, while it was the most obvious symptom of military medievalism in 1914, was not the only one. There were many others: one was the lingering notion of the presence of the monarch on the battlefield. This, though soon to evaporate, was still an acceptable image in the early months of the war. In October 1914, the *News of the World* published a front-page story from the Russian front. It carried the headlines, 'Kaiser's Narrow Escape – Perilous Flight From the Battlefield – The Tsar takes the Field at Head of Mighty Army'. Though the details of the item failed to live up to the promise of the headlines ('It is stated that the Kaiser escaped with difficulty from the field . . .' 'The Tsar has left for the theatre of war . . .') the appearance of the story is in itself an indicator of the spirit of the times.

The medievalism of public and press was perhaps understandable, but there are abundant signs that it did not stop there; it was an attitude that permeated the highest levels. It was one of the most costly errors of assessment in the whole of history.

Writing some fifty years later, war historian Lynn Montross was to observe: 'It was the tragedy of World War I that the century of comparative peace in Europe since Waterloo seemed to have made romanticists out of the professional soldiers who held in their hands the lives of millions of conscript citizens.'

By Christmas 1914 German losses had reached 747,465 killed and wounded; French casualties in the same period were 854,000. The British Expeditionary Force, some 100,000 men, had been virtually wiped out. And now, with the confrontation across no man's land, the professional soldiers faced a problem beyond all expectation. This gigantic stalemate was a position nobody had reckoned with. It was, as the cavalrymen began privately to tell themselves, not like other wars at all.

Here then is the scene: a military caste still deeply committed to the modes of the nineteenth century, with no real idea of the magnitude of the disaster, and no wish, as its significance unfolded, to confess to the world that it had come as a surprise. For each of them, at home, a basically nineteenth-century public; for each of them, at the front, opponents in similar trouble.

Each of the belligerents was concerned only with the validity of his own particular aims, each ignored the possibility of things going wrong; each counted on a short sharp knock-out blow; each failed to understand the chain-reaction effect of multiple alliance; each failed to realize the significance of mobilization plans which, once started, led irreversibly to the logical conclusion of war . . .

In their trenches on a 650-mile front the survivors, now amply reinforced, faced each other across the mud and awaited further instructions.

The generals played a deadpan game. In this unprecedented situation who was to advise them? Who was to question their expertise? More to the point, who would want to reveal the truth? Certainly not one government to another. Certainly not the authorities to the people at home. Who, in any case, in the protective fog of war, was to realize the full extent of their losses? The general were their own accountants.

The generals did the only possible thing; with commendable sang-froid, and with the grim-faced resolution that brought only admiration from those at home, they shovelled more men in. If resources had not been strong enough to force a decision at the beginning, they must be increased until they did. The philosophy of shovelling men in was to remain unquestioned to the end.

The generals had three primary interests: concern for their own reputations, the need to encourage and control the people at home, and the need for a continuing supply of men and material. With these taken care of, the rest of the game was theirs to play. It was, in the main, a confidence trick, a trick in which shaken professionals, playing before an inexpert audience, contrived to bluff their way through the difficult bits. The story of the First World War, with its 30 million killed and wounded, is the story of how they did it.

Throughout the war, the dominant need was for men. On the continent, where conscription was the accepted norm, mobilization summoned millions within days. In each country the conveyor-belt started with the signing of a single document. All able-bodied men, the vast majority already trained in peace-time military service, were automatically called up. The first few days of 1914 saw the massing of a total of some ten million men. The final total was to reach 65 million.

In Britain the case was different. With no conscription, and with a standing army of hardly more than 150,000, the need for more men was urgent. At first there was a rush to volunteer. A wave of patriotic fervour, combined with prospects of an early end to the war, brought many thousands to the enlistment centres. In some areas the machinery of recruitment was overwhelmed. But within a few weeks enthusiasm cooled; numbers turned to a trickle.

Within a few weeks, too, the British Expeditionary Force in France was suffering fearful losses. It became obvious that not only replacements but whole new armies were needed. Soon Kitchener was calling for a million men. From now until 1916, when conscription was finally introduced, the recruitment picture was one of varying forms of moral pressure. As with other pressures in this war, levels started low; as elsewhere, they escalated quickly. Kitchener's final score as recruiting agent was to top the 5,000,000 mark.

(Recruitment was another field in which archaism survived. British official regulations still provided for the payment of a reward to anyone 'who brings a Recruit to a Recruiter, or to a Military Barrack'. In 1914 the going rate was 5s to 2s 6d (12½p to 25p) per head. The payment was in lineal descent from similar rewards paid to press gangs and their henchmen in earlier times. It may be assumed that Kitchener did not qualify.)

Initially the appeal was barely so much as an invitation. One recruiting announcement bore the royal crest and signed off, as customary, with *God Save the King*. Its message was matter-of-fact: *For Those Who Want to Serve Their Country: Men who are medically fit, who are 5ft 3ins high and upwards, whose chest measurement is at least 34ins, can join the Army under the following conditions ...*

Pitched only a notch or two more urgently, and in support of Kitchener's appeal, a recruiting band placard said *Britain's New Army: Complete the Second Half Million – Men Wishing to Join Fall in and Follow the Band.*

Later the tone is less relaxed: *Rally round the flag – To arms, Citizens of the Empire – The Only Road for an Englishman* ... These and other invocations of Britishness are typical of the campaign's second wave.

Soon there is a striving for a new impact. Eric Field, secretary of a voluntary campaign committee, writes:

Pure patriotism as a recruiting appeal soon lost its initial force. We ran the gamut of all the emotions that make men risk their lives–and all the factors that deter them from doing so ...

One well-worked vein was the implication that the reader – and the reader alone – was the odd man out, the only defaulter: *Your friends need you: be a Man!* and *Every Fit Briton should Join our Brave Men at the Front – Enlist Now!* Implications of cowardice were never far behind: *Have you a reason – or only an excuse? It is far better to face the bullets than to be killed at home by a bomb – Join the Army at once and help to stop an air raid.* (This last, a poster illustration of a zeppelin over St Paul's Cathedral, reverted to type with the addition of *God Save the King*.) Zeppelin raids, like the shelling of Scarborough and other towns, provided good recruitment copy.

No opportunity went unused. German atrocities in Belgium, many of them the product of rumour alone, were graphically exploited. Even the New Year, the hopeful dawn of 1915, was used as a recruiting carrot. 'Greetings' posters appeared showing soldiers marching into a glorious sunrise. The caption was: *Victory in 1915 – You can make it certain – Join Now.*

Soon the manpower campaigns were scraping the bottom of the barrel of coercion. Led by the press, public opinion joined in. Clergy preached enlistment from the pulpit;

musical comedy ladies offered kisses for volunteers; women publicly presented white feathers to men not in uniform.

Appeals ranged shallower and deeper. One gambit presented the whole thing as a diversion: *Come on, don't spoil a good fight for want of men to win it!* And another showed a cheery Tommy stepping out, and quoted a passage from a letter from General Sir Horace Smith-Dorrien 'written in the trenches of the Aisne': '*When the order came to advance there were smiling faces everywhere.*' At the other end of the scale there was a harrowing portrayal of a postwar father and his children: '*Daddy*,' they ask of their all-civilian, and now shame-faced parent, '*What did YOU do in the Great War*?' Most memorable however, and most haunting and irritating, was the pointing finger of Kitchener himself, whose sombre gaze and handlebar moustache confronted millions...The finger singled out each straggler individually: *Your country needs YOU.*

Give Your Sons

Some sectors of the market proved specially hard to move. The rustic volunteer particularly, needed more than average pushing. Writing in *The Saturday Review* Lieutenant-Colonel Dudley Buckle bemoans the country recruiter's lot:

For many years I have worked hard . . . by speaking at concerts, by talking to farm lads, and by distributing the literature of the subject. My attempts have been crowned with failure . . . The farmers looked upon me as a harmless lunatic.

I soon became aware that my very good, kind and hospitable friend the farm labourer had not one atom of patriotism in him and knew not the meaning of the word 'Empire'.

Such is the man whom we have asked, begged, entreated and argued with at meetings and casual encounters to 'volunteer' for the defence of his country, which he only now half believes could be invaded.

And with what success? After having travelled many weary miles, having visited thousands of farm cottages, as a would-be recruiter, on my own, I fear I must sadly answer, 'Very, very little'.

But this slackness, this appalling indifference and want of patriotism is by no means confined to my own county. Two short notes of mine in the *Daily Mail* have brought me crowds of letters from all parts of England and from Wales, confirming my opinion, and showing that it is the same in many other countries . . .

The Lieutenant-Colonel confesses that he had distributed in Northumberland and Country Durham 'more than twenty stone of literature', but still the agricultural worker failed to respond. Pointing to the better record of the miner (who, to be sure, he recognizes as having greater economic incentives) he looks to the time when 'one of these exceptions, returning from the wars, will teach their village friends the meaning of the word "patriotism".'

The reluctance of the farm worker gave rise to special recruiting drives. One such campaign utilized a printed notice, in which the recruiting agent expresses his surprise and concern at the lack of response from a given locality. He announces his intention of returning shortly for a further effort. The force of the announcement is only slightly weakened by the fact that the name of the locality, left blank on the notice, is filled in by hand. It would appear that other localities, too, called for a second visit.

Further evidence of special effort appears in leaflets and folders directed specifically to the country man. Many of these, clearly devised for the yokel sector, make memorable reading: One such item, addressed to *The Population of This Parish*, carries a special message from Kitchener and the general title HARK! THE NATION CALLS!! Declaring that 'the People of Our Countryside' are the backbone of the Nation ('and to whom should Kitchener look with more confidence than to our sons of the soil?') it points out that the men who join the New Army may well have some special reason to be proud of it for the rest of their lives. 'They may become famous for valour; they may rise rapidly in the ranks; they may cover themselves and their regiments with glory'. In any case, the reader is reminded, 'they will be honoured for the rest of their lives by their relations and friends and fellow-men generally.' In a major passage, in the heaviest of oversize type, the writer strikes home:

COUNTRYMEN HAVE ALWAYS BEEN BRAVE FIGHTERS. Next year it will be 100 years since they helped the Duke of Wellington to beat Napoleon, the latter of whom endeavoured to crush the civilised peoples and nations of Europe. The Germans are To-day trying to do what Napoleon Tried and Failed to do'. They have jeered at and threatened Great Britain for many years. Now they have to be Crushed, like Napoleon, or every family in this country must be prepared to suffer! We are fighting for our Honour, for our National Existence, and in Defence of Nations weaker than ourselves. Think over these things; then DO YOUR DUTY!

Predictably, the booklet finishes with GOD SAVE THE KING! But there is a rustic-type addendum: AND DOWN WITH EVERY ENEMY OF OUR COUNTRY!!

It must be said that in other quarters recruitment campaigns met with less resistance. Eric Field reports that it was often possible to tell by recruiting figures which appeal succeeded and which failed. 'Once we ran quite a small campaign in Ireland with copy specially directed to Irishmen. Inside a fortnight it trebled recruiting figures in Dublin; in a month it had doubled the rate all over Ireland.'

For the most part, however, it was up-hill work. With ever-diminishing returns, the efforts of the recruiters were redoubled. Within a short time campaign planners began to cast about for reinforcements. They looked to the women. Soon they were appealing to one half of the population to appeal to the other half; they called on the women to bring in the men.

As with the earlier man-to-man approach, the gambit appeared in many guises. But here the mechanics of appeal were less susceptible of camouflage. The message was clear; as one famous poster bluntly put it: *Women of Britain say GO!* (Another poster took the matter a stage further. It showed a women indicating ravished Belgium to her civilian man. *Will you go,* she cries, *or must I?*)

The women of Britain had not been backward in saying GO! from the start. In early September, 1914, the London *Evening News* carried declaration forms to be filled in by female persuaders. These declarations, bearing the curious heading *Women's Service League* [19], committed the signatory to a two-fold undertaking: first, to persuade 'every man I know to offer his services to his country' and second, 'never to be seen in public with any man who . . . has refused to respond to his country's call'. In an article accompanying the printed form Baroness Orczy, founder of the League, makes no bones about the Women's role.

Mothers of English sons, your boy cannot stand aside any longer and let other men do the fighting for him and for you, or he will for ever after be called a craven and a coward, and you, his mother, will be ashamed to look all brave men and women in the face. What English mother is there who would see her son called for ever after by that terrible name 'Coward'?

The women who sang 'Your King and Country Want You' made no bones about the women's role either. In 1914 the song was heard at theatres and music halls all over the country, with such distinguished executants as Maggie Teyte and Phyllis Dare. Nor was Her Majesty Queen Mary unamused. She was 'graciously pleased to make an exception in the case of this song', and accepted its formal dedication to herself.

Also in no two minds were the women who wrote to the papers about 'slackers'. 'The women must do their best and strain every nerve to make their men volunteer, as there is not an hour to be lost to begin their preparation for the front,' wrote one vicarious fighter. 'It simply terrifies me to see the crowds of able-bodied, healthy men of all classes, wherever I go, lounging about with cigarettes or pipes in their mouths . . .'

It was not long before the private enterprise of women received official sponsorship. On September 2 1914 the War Office accepted the offer of 'voluntary women workers' in a house-to-house recruiting canvass throughout the London area. (As to how the women made out at London's front doors, the record is silent.)

Soon the woman-orientated manpower drive got fully under way. Posters appeared: *To the Women of Britain: won't you help and send a man to join the Army today? Is Your 'best Boy' wearing Khaki . . .? Don't pity the girl who is alone – her young man is probably a soldier – fighting for her and her country, and for YOU . . . Think it over, then ask him to join the Army today . . .*

With mounting directness, the campaign closed in on its prey. Taking a leaf (and one or two phrases) out of the Baroness's book, it gave mothers, as well as sweethearts, some pretty straight talk [24]: *Do you expect other mothers' sons to defend you and your sons? Sweethearts: If you cannot persuade him to answer his country's call and protect you now,* DISCHARGE HIM *as unfit!* (The expressions *Enlist now at the nearest recruiting office* and *God Save the King* appear to have got in by an oversight of habit.)

The biggest broadside came from the Mothers' Union. It was a four-page leaflet, and it ran to nearly two thousand words. It was irresistible. Entitled 'To British Mothers', it bore the subtitle 'How they can help enlistment'. It was written by 'one of them' – one whose father had died on the plains of India 'serving against the Mutineers'. It enjoined her sisters to do just two things. The first of these was to pray. The second was to give. The 'give' section was strong:

GIVE YOUR SONS. Day by day the battle rolls on over there in fair France. Day by day gallant Frenchmen and lads fight and fight, and many fall and cover themselves with glory – the glory of unselfish courage: *but they are outnumbered.*

For each Frenchman there are two Germans. Day by day the battle rolls on and by the side of those brave French soldiers stand our own brave men who left us all eager to prove their manhood, and they too fight and fight, and many fall and cover themselves with glory: *but they are outnumbered.* For each Englishman there are two Germans. English mothers gave them, English Mothers from the Queen to the cottager, sending their sailor boys and soldier lads ungrudgingly to live or die for the Country.

But they *may* give in vain, so far as success goes, because NOT ENOUGH MEN ARE SENT OUT, AND THIS LARGELY BECAUSE NOT ENOUGH MOTHERS SAY TO THEIR SONS, AS ONE DID LATELY, '*My boy, I don't want you to go, but if I were you I should go*'.

In her peroration the writer speaks of the role of the mother – 'the right sort of Mother for Old England' – called to brace on the armour of her sons 'just as truly as the ladies of old braced on the armour of their knights'. She recalls the loss of her father ('I have known personally what it costs to give one's best and dearest for one's country') and commends such sacrifice to her sisters. She signs off to a background of heavenly choirs:

Your own hearts, now so torn with the parting, will beat high one day with thankfulness and pride when you see your lad come back from the hard-won victory he has helped to win for his Country; or, if God has another plan for him, and like so many another English Mother you must hear that he has given his life for his Country, you will have a yet deeper cause for thankfulness that he is among the long roll of English heroes, ever to be held in highest honour while the English name lasts, and better – far better even that that – the welcome of the King of Kings will greet him–'*Well done, good and faithful servant, enter thou into the joy of thy Lord.*'

Yes, we may think of each brave soldier so. He has died doing his Duty. Christ Who sees the heart, receives such, whether they lie down patiently under weary sickness, or fall on the battlefield.

And we Mothers can only pray and strive to follow our heroes' brave example, and DO OUR DUTY . . .

When conscription came in 1916, the appeal to women as intermediaries faded. Now, instead of seeking women as recruiting agents, the government sought them for themselves – as recruits. As the gaps in the ranks of the men at the front increased, as greater numbers of men were drawn from civilian life to replace the losses, women were called to replace the replacements. In the ephemera and memorabilia of the time the theme of women's service becomes increasingly dominant.

Women Go to War

The change of role was crucial. It was also, in the truest sense, epoch-making. The early 1900s had seen mounting militancy in the drive for women's emancipation. It was a minority movement, and for the most part it had proved abortive. With the advent of war it had fallen silent. Now, however, without effort on their part, women found their freedom – not as a concession but as an urgent patriotic duty. The image of the nineteenth century female, the fragile, twittering feather-brain of yesterday, became the munition worker, the bus conductor, the butcher and baker of today. For women as a whole, though war brought unheard-of misery, it also brought unheard-of opportunity. In their overalls, dungarees and boiler suits, they looked back incredulously to their pre-war world; for the first time they had their own pay packets, their own independent existence. It was extraordinary, now that some of them came to think of it, that they had not had it before.

By the end of 1916 large sections of Europe's essential services were staffed by women; one third of workers in the munitions factories were women. It must be recorded that in Britain male resentment of 'dilution of industry' (in which men's jobs were taken over by women) gave way in turn to female resentment of females. 'Educated women' [27], brought in to boost munitions output, were seen by their newly installed sisters as threats to steady jobs. The intruders' services were restricted to Saturdays and Sundays, days which 'women of the leisured class' could sacrifice more readily than working women could. They were called in not to compete with 'the ordinary wage-earner' but to keep things going while she had a weekend off.

The female invasion of industry was common to all the belligerents. In shell manufacture, particularly, women moved in. Britain's poster *Women are Doing their Bit* [78] had its counterpart elsewhere; shell-filling women gazed sternly from the bill-boards from Pittsburg to Vladivostock.

On the land too, women did men's jobs. In transport, distribution and a score of hitherto male preserves, they broke with the past. In Britain, Germany and France they even entertained hopes of getting the vote. (They got it in Britain – those over 30 – in 1918. In Germany it was the year after. Frenchwomen were to wait another 30 years.)

In many countries women got into the fighting services too, serving as auxiliaries and uniformed helpmates. In theory they were subject to the same military discipline as men, but it was noticed that few if any among the various military authorities implemented their right to court-martial a woman for desertion.

Only in nursing was the female role familiar. Here too, in slogans of a score of languages she figured as a universal image. Just as the soldier was the international hero-figure, so was the nurse the heroine of the whole world. Most nations ran their 'Thank Our Nurses' flag-day, all encouraged and applauded her. Britain's nurse-on-the-battlefield greeting card [170] with its clear-cut caption and romanticized image, could have appeared in a score of countries. In the majority of countries the nurse was a near-religious symbol. In Canada the image reached it apotheosis in 'The Greatest Mother in the World', a poster presentation that was to endure into World War II; the picture showed a monumental Red Cross nurse with a diminutive stretcher-case cradled in her arms. America had her popular song-hit, 'Rose of No Man's Land' [229] ('God in his mercy has sent her') and in Italy a postcard nurse [164] knelt unashamedly in the ward in a prayer for victory.

The new status of woman did not prevent her continued work in ordinary do-gooding (she was the heart and soul of most of the world's war charities) or her use as a propaganda motivation symbol. As Britannia, Germania, Marianne de France and other national mother-figures, she came up on posters everywhere.

In ephemera she was widely present. She appeared on charity stamps [169], as whole-page magazine studies [98], as postcard dreams of home [119] and, particularly in Italy, as somnambulous glory-figures, with troops following in her steps [82].

As in peacetime, both before and since, the female figure was found to provide a reliable basis for almost any argument. As mother, nurse, nun or sex-object; as promise, admonition, standard-bearer or reminder, governments used her as a handy all-purpose instrument of war.

There was, however, another aspect to the public attitude to women. Whereas the image was safe from depradation, the woman herself was not. Now out and about in the world of men, the woman herself posed problems that had never been faced before — not, at least, on the extravagant scale of total war.

For all her gallantry and enterprise, in truth the woman of 1914 was ill-equipped to cope with the outside world. The little she knew of the facts of life was a guilty gleaning in a conspiracy of silence. As in her grandmother's time large numbers of women remained ignorant until marriage — some until quite a while after it. (Contraception, menstruation, masturbation, venereal disease — to all but a small minority at opposite ends of the social scale, such matters were taboo. For the citizen of the later twentieth century, it may be difficult to imagine how rigidly the prohibition operated. In a book entitled *Personal Hygiene for Girls,* published in 1914, there are sections on diet, posture, clothing, exercise and similar topics but, apart from 'Constipation', no mention whatsoever of the existence of life below the waist. A short section on 'The Body as a Heritage' remainds the reader that the girls of today 'are the women — the possible mothers, of tomorrow'. For the rest there is a respectable silence.)

With the sudden removal of restraint — with, for the first time, men and women encountering each other on terms of heterogeneous informality, it was not surprising that the facts of life asserted themselves. In every country 'misbehaviour' was a national, though largely covert, talking point. Civil and military authorities became seriously concerned with the mounting threat of venereal disease. In all armies 'health education' became a standard feature of military training.

On the home front, voluntary societies tried to keep an eye on girls in the big cities. Their concern was not only for the girl who was anxious to keep out of trouble but for the girl who was not. In Britain there appeared a Women's Patrol, a semi-official female 'watch and ward'. At railway stations and garrison areas, particularly at night, the patrol moved among crowds, discouraging casual contact. It was not the most popular of wartime innovations. It spent much of its time in countering charges of social espionage.

In similar vein, though less of a target for hostility, was the Women's League of Honour [37]. This was primarily a temperance organization, but its strong parenthesis of sexual purity aligned it clearly as an adjunct to the street patrol. A specifically war-orientated organization, the League saw war conditions as a special threat to chastity and temperance. Its call for 'prayer, purity and temperance', like so many other war commitments, must be taken as applying 'for the duration' only.

Alcohol was a major problem. Military authorities in all countries had for centuries adopted an ambivalent attitude to drink. Drink rations of one sort or another had materially assisted the fighting spirit both in war and peace; on the other hand, drink had made for indiscipline. By the same token, deprived civilians had found comfort in drink; for civil authorities too there had been a fine balance between indulgence and restraint. In 1914, however, all authorities saw the dangers; the triple alliance of drink, indiscipline and disease was too serious a threat to ignore.

In Britain, only one week after the outbreak of war, the city of Norwich was obliged to put out an appeal for moderation in the amount of drink given to the troops by appreciative citizens [12]. Soon public houses opening hours were curtailed and the 'No Treating' law [31] sought to put an end to the bar-room practice whereby each member of a drinking group in turn bought a round of drinks for the whole number. (The habit entailed each member of the group taking as many drinks as there were members of the group; larger and larger wartime groups had led to correspondingly increased intake.) Drinking on troop trains was forbidden. There were serious proposals to stop women drinking in bars. In Russia the sale of vodka was totally prohibited. In France a vigorous anti-drink campaign put out posters and leaflets. In Britain, Buckingham Palace pledged itself to take no more drink for the duration.

It was in its influence on promiscuity that the drink problem was specially feared. Large numbers of women and girls were attracted to training and garrison areas, and the facility of a pub at every street corner was exploited to the full. 'The greatest evil to contend against', said a London clergyman, 'is the waywardness of the poorer class girls, who in nine cases out of ten scorn their mothers' advice.'

The wives of the Archbishop of Canterbury and the Bishops of Southwark and Rochester for their part offered suggestions on how women and girls could help the men of the services:

1 You can work for them in your spare time.
2 You can pray for them.
3 You can help them by expecting them to be steady and brave and good men.
    Many a man has been kept good by thinking of the good straight girl he knows at home who expects him to be good and straight. He is fighting for us women and for our homes. Give him something nice and good and true to think about. Don't let your excitement make you silly and lead you to wander aimlessly about. Remember that war is a very solemn thing. For the men and lads who are learning to take their part in it it is a matter of life and death. Be careful that, so far as you are concerned no one of them shall carry away with him as his last remembrance of England anything but what is pure and gentle and straight and true.

These suggestions were backed up by an appeal from a number of clergymen, who called on women and girls of all ranks and employment to exercise 'reserve and restraint'.

To men, an appeal came from Kitchener himself. In a 'confidential message' to the troops (100,000 copies were printed) the general called for good behaviour in France and Belgium [38]. The message contained, as well as a gratuitous condemnation of looting, a warning as to women, with an oblique reference to disease:

Your duty cannot be done unless your health is sound. So keep constantly on your guard against any excesses. In this new experience you may find temptations both in wine and women. You must entirely resist both temptations, and, while treating all women with perfect courtesy, you should avoid any intimacy.

The general's qualms were well-founded. British army statistics for 1912 had shown that the number of men 'constantly sick' with venereal disease (that is to say, 'off the strength') was 7 per thousand. Extrapolated to 1914 conditions, an army of four million men would give a loss 'off the strength' of some 25,000 men — the equivalent of more than a complete division. Even these figures appear moderate against a Royal Commission's findings for the civilian population; an official estimate of the commissioners put the number of persons in large towns who had been infected with syphillis as one in ten. For gonorrhoea the figure was higher. And the commissioners reported that of all the blindness in Britain, one quarter was caused by gonorrhoea.

With official plans now laid for a three-to-four-year war, it was clear that of the millions of men under arms few were likely to resist temptation, either in wine or women. In all armies provision was made for the recognizing of authorized brothels, medically controlled and supervised. In Britain each embarking soldier now received an additional time of war equipment — a 'prophylactic packet' for his protection behind the lines.

The *American Manual of Military Training* (1917) made a valiant effort: 'The best way to avoid venereal disease is to keep away from lewd women, and live a clean moral life . . . The natural sex impulse can be kept under control by avoiding associations, conversations, and thoughts of a lewd character . . . Seek good companions like your mother and sister . . .' But the manual recognized that some might fail to find such companions. These should use the prophylactic measures as required by the War Department.

Civilian conditions worsened rapidly. The Bishop of London, addressing a crowd outside St James's Piccadilly on his return from a brief visit to the front [103] was moved to compare the gallantry of the Londoner in uniform with those who remained in the capital as *souteneurs* — 'male hawks who walk up and down this very Piccadilly night by night with twenty or thirty helpless and trembling girls under their surveillance, and who take from them the very money the girls earn by their shame . . .' His talk, afterwards published as a book, was a compendious denunciation of war-time morals. It had little or no effect.

What had considerably more effect, particularly on the helpless and trembling girls, was the Defence of the Realm Act's regulation 40D, known familiarly as DORA 40D. The Defence of the Realm Act, a major item of war legislation, comprised some hundreds of separate regulations. These dealt with virtually everything from signalling to the enemy to shops' opening hours. Regulation 40D dealt with venereal disease; it made its transmission by a woman a criminal act: 'No woman who is suffering from venereal disease in a communicable form shall have sexual intercourse with any member of His Majesty's Forces . . .'

The terms of the act featured as title-piece to protest leaflets put out by the Independent Women's Social and Political Union [28], who bitterly resented the placing of the burden of responsibility for transmission of disease on women alone and, among other matters, pointed out that medical inspection of prostitutes would tend to 'legalize vice' and would in any case induce a false sense of security among errant males. They advocated Kitchener's principle. The soldiers, they said, need only be taught to protect themselves by self-control.

The theme of self-control is recurrent in the moral documents of the war. However great the excesses of men in battle, however extravagantly they slaughter each other 'out there', the matter of sex requires calm and restraint. The American YMCA, equally insistent on the decencies, extends its strictures to vocabulary. In a leaflet entitled *Arguments Against the Use of Obscene Language* it invokes the image of the soldier's mother (*Don't use language your mother would blush to hear*). It enumerates five reasons for restraint [181]. Among the list, in passing, appears the threat of venereal disease – and the fact that 'smutty jokes appeal to the brute nature'.

The Independent Women's Social and Political Union, though reserving its opinion on the matter of obscene language, made no bones about DORA 40D. As an organization whose genealogy linked it closely to the movement for women's suffrage, it was a predictable feature of the landscape of protest. Its attitude was to be echoed in a stand against similar anti-VD legislation in World War II.

But the independent social and political women were by no means alone in the expression of dissent in the war. Openly or otherwise, and in spite of impressions of unanimity conveyed by each of the contending governments, minority groups survived. Each country had its quota of anti-war opinion. Each had its no-conscription lobby and its conscientious objectors, officially recognized or not. Each, according to its notion of civil liberties, adopted attitudes to these phenomena.

In Australia a satirical leaflet urged workers to follow the example of their bosses: *To arms, capitalists, parsons, politicians, landlords, newspaper editors and other stay-at-home patriots. Your country needs you in the trenches. Workers, follow your masters!* The printer and publisher of this item was convicted of 'circulating statements likely to prejudice recruiting'. He was sentenced to a fine of £50, with an alternative of six months imprisonment with hard labour.

In Dublin, official talk of the introduction of conscription was countered by mini-proclamations: *Anti-Conscription Pledge: Denying the right of the British Government to enforce compulsory service in this country, we pledge ourselves solemnly to one another to resist conscription by the most effective means at our disposal.*

In Paris a poster announced a meeting at which Alcide Henri du Thil was to reveal means whereby obstacles placed in the way of war inventors could be eliminated and the war thus brought to a successful conclusion in two or three months. The poster named the Council of Ministers and the President of the Republic as instigators of the 'administrative obstructions'. The poster was seized and the meeting did not take place.

As the realities of war emerged, scepticism and opposition increased. By 1917 protests, strikes and, finally, in the forces of a number of the belligerents, mutiny had appeared. In Russia, defection mounted to a conclusion; a printed circular from the Russian Prisoners of War Help Committee in London [202] marks the occasion; the committee begs to inform its subscribers that 'in view of recent developments it finds it necessary to close its operations for the Russian prisoners . . .'

By 1917 the image of a nineteenth-century war could be sustained only with difficulty. Too many people had heard, seen and done too much. But, as though stuck in a groove of unreality, the themes of the image-makers tended to persist. In advertising particularly the war continued to appear as a clean, well-organized adventure. Battlefields stayed green with grass, shells popped harmlessly overhead, and smiling soldiers sat on campstools in the sunshine writing home for more shaving cream.

Typical of the genre was an early showcard for 'Golden Dawn' cigarettes: soft-hatted soldiers in a moorland ditch await the next phase of an exciting action; a genial sergeant scans the horizon for the enemy as he offers the men his open cigarette case. The caption, *Time for one more,* provides a crowning touch of unreality [66]. In similar vein, Dri-Ped, 'the super-leather for soles', presents a healthy soldier group striding over rough country: the headline, *Dri-Ped makes easier the road to Berlin* offers a view of the Western Front that must have intrigued the men in the trenches. This advertisement appeared not in the first few days of 1914, when advertisers might have been forgiven their idyllics, but in the following year, when mud and immobility had set in in earnest.

(The 'clean' image of the advertisers was sharply at variance with the soldiers' image of themselves. Conditions in the trenches became so appalling that, for many, the only escape was humour. The 'Ole Bill' image was by no means exclusive to Britain [153,157].)

One advertisement that did fail to survive the first few weeks of the war, and which, more than any other single item, expresses the innocent expectations of 1914, was for the 'Rider's Joy'. This German marvel — 'a boon to every cavalryman in the field' — was a 'heatable stirrup', final touch of luxury for the modern fighting man. 'Obtainable everywhere, or direct from the sole manufacturers. Price, per pair, 11.50 marks complete with charcoal.' [85]

Not far removed was Germany's 'Feist Feldgrau' showcard [104] in which an officer, glass in hand, smiles from the battlement of a medieval fortress. And for grandiose naivety, few items can surpass the compendious Selfridge announcement [17] in which the public is offered not only windows full of flagged maps and other war facilities but free lessons in the making of garments for the Soldier and Sailor on Active Service, and on the roof, free use of a firing range for rifle practice. At much the same time Germany's national magazine *Jugend* announces, under the heading 'Iron Christmas' [13] that the cover picture for its approaching yuletide issue will show 'Germania, more lovely than ever ... decking a good old Christmas tree with Iron Crosses and little coloured lights ...'

Bread and Money; Blood and Iron

Wartime advertising could be divided into three groups. The first two jumped unmistakably on the bandwagon of war: there was the naive approach (smiling soldiers and moorland battlefields), and there was the don't-worry-it-may-never-happen approach, which played frankly on fears of death and disaster. The third group, a minority, contrived to ignore the war entirely. Drawing its strength from a refusal to concede that anything untoward was happening, it offered elegance and luxury as usual: *The Riding Burberry ... for riding side-saddle as well as astride ... exceedingly graceful straightfronted appearance when mounted ...*

The fear-inducing group was easily the most significant. Unfettered by ethical or government control, advertisers first roused, and then affected to assuage, fears of every kind. Dangers were multiple: air-raids, German bullets, gas attacks; sexual rejection through debility, neuralgia, spotty complexion; death by drowning at sea — these and many other hazards were diligently catered for: *The Pianola Piano ... Better for the folks at home than thinking about Zeppelins ... His first leave for fourteen months—such a lot of things they'd hoped to do and say—and she helpless and miserable through a sudden attack of neuralgia ... A well-known lady passenger and her maid rescued from the torpedoed "Persia" ... telegraphed last week to friends in London* SAVED BY GRIEVE'S WAISTCOAT ...

Typical of this genre, and mincing no matters, was the gasmask advertisement in the

Paris papers [80]; *At any moment the Zeppelins may come. The German dirigibles carry gas bombs . . .*

Some advertisers, on the other hand, jumped on the bandwagon less intrusively. A military maxim of von Moltke (*War is an element in God's natural order*) was given away as a dug-out pin-up by a German cigarette company; the firm's name appeared on it only in the smallest possible print. Similarly, 'Dr Gentner's Snow Powder' [86] contented itself with only a nominal mention in a showcard seascape.

On the whole, however, the role of the advertiser was less than glorious. We may note in passing the trade advertisement for one of the munition-making products of the Cleveland Automatic Machine Company in 1916 [84]: *This shell is more effective than the regular shrapnel ... fragments become coated with these acids ... and wounds caused by them mean death in terrible agony . . .*

We may also note the unabated flood of advertising for medical and pharmaceutical preparations:

Sanatogen provides a power reserve on which overtaxed nerve and body resources may draw. For our soldiers it offers an unequalled potential for the maintaining of health and powers of resistance . . . Available in special Field Service Pack at all chemists . . . [91]

I have been out here since October 1915 and a few weeks ago I began to feel the strain of days and nights of Active Service I felt tired and worn out . . . I had a wretched time until one of the boys got a bottle of Phosferine sent out to me . . . It has quite pulled me together until the danger of collapse has passed away . . .

It must be observed however that the state of medical knowledge, even at the less popular levels, was not reassuring. The medical profession was scarcely out of the herbalist stage. It has been said that some two-thirds of the medicines of 1914 were substances in daily use by the physicians of the Middle Ages. The rest were latter-day palliatives. There were no antibiotics, virtually no x-ray services and no blood supplies. Battle wounds (even without the assistance of the Cleveland Automatic Machine Company) became infected almost as a matter of course. Over half of the casualties with stomach injuries died of infection. 'Died of Wounds' was an all-too-frequent – and inaccurate – epitaph.

Infestation by mites and lice [228,230] brought 'trench fever'; winter brought frostbite [149]. These afflictions, like 'shellshock' (the military term for nervous breakdown) were relatively trival; all were the subject of pioneering work in the newly galvanized research laboratories and hospitals of the belligerents. Much of it held high promise for the future.

But for the sick and wounded at the time the outlook was not good. Even at the level of ordinary hospital nursing, however gallant and self-sacrificing, techniques were still embryonic. Among the first 'war' publications to be advertised in Britain in 1914 was a reprint of *Notes on Nursing* [167], by Florence Nightingale ('of Crimea fame').

Apart from those who lived in the actual battle zones, ordinary people in most countries saw the war in its early stages as a thing apart – a spectacle more or less distant, more or less separate and self-contained. But reality slowly intruded. In each country the German concept of 'the nation at war' – the total dedication of entire populations – took over. For the first time, warfare was not merely a matter for the armed forces: civilian was at war with civilian. And for the first time civilians far removed from the firing line were at risk from air attack. More than that: for the first time the whole body of the population was viewed as a legitimate target for the infliction of privation and, if necessary, starvation.

Mutual attempts at blockade, coupled with internal shortages caused by extravagance in war production, brought home economies to chaos. Goods became scarce. Prices went up. Pressures on the civilian mounted month by month. Shortage, initially viewed as a nuisance, soon became an all-pervading preoccupation. Among the ephemera and memorabilia of the war the theme of shortage appears increasingly dominant. It ranges over a broad spectrum from the discipline of food rationing to the rigours experienced by customers of the Sandow Corset Company [194].

Rationing schemes, most of them remarkably similar in detail, were a feature of the home front almost everywhere [52–59]. So were exhortations to economy [174,176]. So were devices for evading restrictions, and prosecutions for infractions.

In most countries meatless days and 'war recipes' encouraged food encomy. In America, were food restrictions promised greater shipments to allies and fighting forces, a campaign theme was *Eat less Wheat, Meat, Fats and Sugar*. In France the message was much the same (the *Eat Less Meat* slogan of a schoolchild's poster makes the point [190]) and in Britain His Majesty issued his belt-tightening proclamation (page 10). In Germany the potato achieved the status of a national hero [191]. Most countries organized the collection of unconsidered trifles. Germany, hardest pressed, set up collection schemes for apple and pear peelings, acorns and chestnuts, fruit-stones for oil production. Leaflets, press advertisements and posters called not only for spare edibles but for salvaged metal oddments – aluminium, copper, brass, nickel and tin – and for bottles, paper, and even human hair.

By the end of 1917 people in some German areas were being obliged to render returns in a chicken-census [195]. 'The greatest economy is the holiest duty,' said Germany's 'Wall of Steel' appeal [177]; 'this war will be won not only with blood and iron but with bread and money ...' These were the conditions that gave rise to the German substitute industry; *ersatz* foods – cakes from clover meal and chestnuts, coffee from barley, chicory and figs. Food substitutes became commonplace. For hungry people they became even edible.

For civilians everywhere economy was one of the key-words of the war. In Britain the newspapers for November 11, 1918, Armistice Day, carried Board of Trade injunctions to save coal: 'Take the coal *off* the fire when you go to bed ... The coal you save today will start your fire tomorrow ...' Shortage was destined to carry over into peace, as well.

A corollary of shortage was inflation. The archive shows steadily rising prices as a continuing theme. At first there are references to modest rises – a halfpenny here, a penny there. Sometimes the rises are effected by stealth; the stick-on label, concealing yesterday's price, is applied to the product package or to advertising material. (Britain's 'Sea King' item is typical [180]: price panels on the showcard, invisible to the casual glance, updated the price by a halfpenny.) More often, especially when the increase is too big to escape notice, new prices are formally announced. Sometimes there is an apology, sometimes not. A red-printed slip from the Town Hall, Hampstead, in June 1916 advises of a 'war charge' of $33\frac{1}{3}$ per cent on all accounts for electricity; 'by order, Arthur P Johnson, Town Clerk'. Message ends.

Britain's pattern of inflation was typical. Food prices had risen at the outbreak of war by some 18 per cent. A year later the level had risen to 45 per cent. By the end of the war it was 133 per cent and the general cost of living stood at 125 per cent. In Germany, however, the pattern was destined to run wild; the rising spiral ultimately priced a newspaper at one million million marks.

As part of a desperate attempt to stabilize the economy and to acquire foreign currency, the authorities called on the population for donations of precious metals. In exchange for gifts of gold, donors received vouchers valid for use in payment of local taxes [179]. In some cases 'iron' watch chains were offered for gold ones.

Uncle Sam Wants You

When America entered the war on April 6 1917 the condition of all of the combatants was parlous. In spite of the collapse of Russia as a fighting force, the deadlock in the West remained unbroken. Exhaustion, bankruptcy – and above all irreparable losses in manpower – had brought the armies to a mutually paralyzing stranglehold. The territories over which they had been fighting had become a meaningless mire. Home-front support on all sides was flagging. Soldiers had forgotten, if they had ever known, what they were fighting about: all that they sought, under an apparently interminable two-way rain of bombardment, was personal survival.

The coming of a million or more fresh American troops to the Western Front was the signal, on all sides, for a last desperate effort. But the Americans took a long time getting there. An army of some 150,000 men, trained only for sub-tropical skirmishes on the Mexican border, needed a radical rethink. By the end of the year, fewer than 200,000 men had arrived and there had still been no major action involving Americans It was to be the middle of 1918 before the United States had shovelled on its first million soldiers. By the end of the war the US total of mobilized men was to reach $4\frac{1}{2}$ million.

As with the Europeans before her, manpower was America's chief concern. The archive conveys the story [108,109]. But whereas on the continent of Europe the gathering of men had been a purely administrative matter, and whereas in Britain it had at least started as a process of cajolement, in America it was complicated by being both at once. Parallel with enlistment by registration and ballot, voluntary recruitment compaigns cajoled and persuaded. The pointing finger, successful all over Europe, was now slotted on to Uncle Sam. Inevitably, there were clashes of interest. Men volunteering from industry left war-production lines in disarray. Those who replaced them, often untrained and unskilled, were snatched away by the draft. Soon the zeal of the enlistment campaigners had to be curtailed. In September 1918, volunteering was stopped altogether. As with all other countries in the fight, centralized control took over. July 1917 had seen Government control of food and fuel. In December it was the railways. Other controls followed quickly. By the middle of 1918 the inviolable rights of the American citizen had become as tenuous as those of the British, French, Italians and Germans. The Americans, too, adopted the principle of 'the nation in arms', and the modes and methods of Europe moved in.

So too with money: the war-bond technique, perennial standby of the European belligerents, went American. Through high-powered publicity and all the techniques of a rapidly developing public-relations and promotion industry, the American Government persuaded the American people to lend it money. But where Europe had merely tinkered with the idea, America went all out.

Government loan campaigns became minor industries. At mass meetings, parades and stage presentations, celebrities called for cash and more cash. They got it. When the Fourth Liberty Loan was floated in 1918 it was calculated that over half the nation's adult population had subscribed. The 'Honor Button' for citizens [105] and the 'Honor Flag' for fully subscribing cities, were nationally accepted emblems.

'Honor' was a good word in America in 1917 and 1918. When President Wilson announced the setting up of 'registers' of men available for military service, he prudently called them 'Honor Lists'. The point was significant: the last time conscription had appeared on the American scene – in the Civil War, 1863 – there had been bloody riots, with some 100 draft officials actually murdered by unwilling conscripts.

In America, perhaps more than anywhere else, the woman's role as recruiting agent shone forth. *Gee, I wish I were a man ...*' said one poster pin-up – herself, alas, unable to fight. Said another, usurping the role of father figure. *I want you for the Navy*. And more simply, more frankly, a working-class American mom hands over her all-American son to Uncle Sam in person: *Here he is, Sir ...* [111].

Europe's 'Britannia' figures – Germania, Italia, Marianne de France and the rest – had a re-run, this time as 'America', 'Liberty' or 'Honor', sometimes as all three in one. As everywhere, the female form did yeoman service. On the commercial level, Hart Schaffner and Marx (Makers of Good Clothes) latched on with a suitably illustrated quote from General Pershing [114]. Whatever the level, whatever the message, there was nothing like a dame.

Among the many familiar ingredients in the American mix was shortage. Economies, not only in food, but in raw materials for industry, became vital. As Germany's U-boat war intensified and war production accounted for more and more of internal supplies, prices rose. Disruption of industry through enlistment put labour costs up. The discovery by the Ingersoll Company that the dollar watch now had to be sold for $1.35 was typical. Shocked, the nation nevertheless carried on.

Coal became short. Production needs for 1918 were 80 million tons more than for 1917. In spite of productivity appeals, final figures fell short of this by 60 million. Transport became short. In spite of appeals for load-spreading [193], winter coal delivery facilities became overloaded while summer ones were neglected.

Though America's war was to last only some sixteen months compared with a total of four and a half years for the others, its effects on her home economy were in many ways as telling as they had been for the rest of the combatants. As in Europe, people began to see that things would never be quite the same again; the day of the dollar watch was fading fast.

Following Instructions

For the civilian everywhere, conditions were bad. For the man in the firing line they were far beyond the ordinary limits of human endurance. Here the archive can only hint at the truth. But at least the soldier, unlike the civilian, had his instructions. For the majority in the trenches, bereft of illusion, idealism or much else in the way of incentive, this was all they had.

'On the approach of poisonous gases,' said the respirator instruction card issued from British GHQ in 1915, 'open the respirator and place the cotton waste pad over the mouth and nose, grasping it with the teeth to keep it in position ... After it has been in use for some time, move the respirator to one side or the other so as to breathe through new portions of the cotton waste ... When the respirator no longer stops the entrance of the gas, apply a fresh one ...'

In March 1917 the instructions were different [220]; the respirator was different. So were the gases. Phosgene, and other mixes, had arrived. Observed the text books [222]: 'The passage of the vapour down the respiratory tract may cause such severe injury to the living mucous membranes of the trachea and bronchioles that they are eventually destroyed and sloughed away ...' The instruction card, however, insisted on optimism. 'You have nothing to fear from a gas attack,' it said, '(a) if your respirator or helmet is in good order ... (b) if you remain calm and carry out the measures in which you have been instructed ...' Gas casualties in the war totalled nearly one million men.

For bayonet fighting too, there were instructions. 'If possible [126], the point of the bayonet should be directed against an opponent's throat ... Four to six inches penetration is sufficient to incapacitate and allow for quick withdrawal, whereas if a bayonet is driven home too far it is often impossible to withdraw...' It was reported that in British army attacks on the Western Front, raw recruits were heard mechanically yelling training commands as they fought: 'In... Out ... On guard.'

There were instructions for all eventualities. All of the military manuals were agreed as to the undesirability of having soldiers stop fighting to look after casualties. Most of them merely prohibited the practice, But the United States manual left the reader in no doubt whatever:

When officers or men belonging to fighting troops leave their proper place to carry back, or to care for, wounded during the progress of the action, they are guilty of skulking. This offense must be repressed with the utmost vigor.

Burial of the dead was conceded to give rise to occasional trouble. Some instruction books recommended that where possible men should not be obliged to inter the bodies of their personal friends. But most such items had to be radically modified for Western Front conditions. Bodies lay often for weeks, sometimes for months, under fire in no man's land. British Field Regulations, updated to 1917, made the point: 'Bodies in a state of putrefaction lying out in advance of the trenches, which cannot be buried or cremated owing to hostile fire, or bodies uncovered in parapets of trenches where they have been hastily buried often give rise to considerable nuisance...' Instructions for dealing with the matter were explicit [123].

Details of mass cremation also appear. But burial is preferred: '... a layer of stones or brushwood is placed at the bottom and the bodies are laid across in 3 or 4 superposed rows to a distance of not less than three feet from the surface... In times of pressure, pits may be of greater depth, even as much as 40 feet... Clothing may be left on the body, but it tends to retard dissolution, and if rapidity in this respect is desired, as much of the clothing as possible should be removed before burial...'

The First World War was a succession of 'times of pressure'. Death piled on death, till men became inured to it. The diary of Captain Reginald Leetham [124] bears witness. After telling of the 'great big Hun' whose face is trampled in the mud by one of Leetham's brother officers, the diary continues:

Then they [the British] found a great big underground dugout and threw a dozen bombs in. The yells and groans were awful to begin with, but all was silent after six bombs were thrown in. When Murray and his men entered and flashed their torchlights, they found about 30 dead Germans in various positions... They brought back five wounded Huns as prisoners for our Staff to get information from, but half way across four of them turned sullen and refused to walk further, so our men left their bodies where they shot them...

Later the diary describes another action. Afterwards:

I continually picked up water bottles from dead men. Altogether I suppose I distributed about 30 of these... The trench was a horrible sight. It was wider than my part and the dead were stretched out on one side on top of each other 6 high – literally. There were twice the number of dead men than live ones. As the day went on it got hotter and hotter. I thought at the time I should never get rid of the peculiar disgusting smell of the vapour of warm human blood. I would rather have smelt gas a hundred times... To do one's duty one was continually climbing over corpses in every position...

In June 1918 the lady columnist of *The Tatler* commented on the morale of the soldiers and their understandable distaste for the war:

How weary they grow of it all – even those who went to war straight from school and have never known a world that wasn't a war-world. No one seems to think it can end for another year or so, and the prospect – on 2 ounces of tea per week – *is* appalling, isn't it?

In the end, as though by common consent, all of the belligerents stopped feeding casualty lists to the press. Like mourning, which had also been unanimously discouraged, the statistics of dead and wounded were felt to be bad for morale. In Britain a brief statement announced that 'owing to the limitation of space imposed by the shortage of paper' full press lists would no longer be available. But anyone who cared to could subscribe to His Majesty's *Weekly Casualty List* (60 pages in the issue for October 16 1918 [219]), price threepence per copy. Not available for publication where the sector-by-sector figures [216] prepared daily behind the lines at GHQ.

When the final cease-fire order came on November 11 1918 [232], dead and wounded had notched up 14,000,000 for Germany and Austria, 9,000,000 for Russia, 6,000,000 for France, 3,000,000 for the British Empire, and 350,000 for the United States. Italy, Turkey, Bulgaria, Serbia and the rest brought the total to 37,494,186. More than half the total number mobilized had become casualties.

Today in the 1970s, as the generation of the survivors begins to pass, witnesses fall silent. We are left with war graves, memorials and history books. And now, as a last memento we have the collected trivia of the time, the cuttings, souvenirs and printed oddments of the world's first multi-million massacre. They cover a wide spectrum: prisoners' parcels and the Red Cross; censorship and spy mania; children's games and toys; cartoons and caricatures – the archive omits no facet of the story.

But there is an additional factor, in its way as deadly as the casualty statistics – an ingredient new to the world at the time, but today familiar. In the printed forms and orders, the enlistment and requisition notices, the ration books and instruction sheets – in the documents of management and control we see the true beginnings of the centralized society. Never before had so many millions of human beings been brought to do what they were told to do; never before had they massed and fought so obediently; never had control – of civilian and soldier alike – been more complete.

Succeeding generations took up where 1918 had left off: it was the beginning of a new era in social engineering.

The First World War contrived not only to introduce the concept of Total Control, but to secure its almost universal acceptance. Of the many unforeseen side-effects of the war, this is perhaps the most long-lasting and far-reaching.

In this, as in virtually every other respect, the war brought a catastrophic change in the level of human affairs. The story reveals a clearly perceptible discontinuity – an irreparable break in the continuum of history. The nineteenth century may be said to have stopped at the Battle of the Somme; but more than that: as we look back through the curtain of the war we see a whole historical epoch, a civilization, now beyond recall. The First World War marks the end of the innocence of the ordinary man.

MAURICE RICKARDS

January 1975

SEEING IN THE NEW YEAR.

CELEBRATIONS AT LONDON HOTELS.

ELABORATE PROGRAMMES.

In the London celebrations of the passing of the old year and the coming of the new the large hotels and restaurants formed, as usual, the centre of attraction, and most of them were so crowded last night that late comers

Cecil, 900; and several other places from 200 to 400. The Trocadero was also well patronized.

SCENIC EFFECTS.

The demand for scenic effects at these entertainments grows each year, and although lowered lights with a fanfare of trumpets are still used at midnight, some striking tableau or other novelty is usually added. The Hôtel Métropole usually shows enterprise on such occasions, and last night proved no exception. A very varied programme was begun after 9 o'clock, including dances of every description, to say nothing of the farandole. The grand tableau at midnight

At the Waldorf the tables were decorated with miniature dirigible airships, on one side of which was printed "The Waldorf Hotel" and on the other "1913." These were released and sailed away into space as the lights went out at the stroke of 12. On the lights being turned on once more an enormous pie embellished with swans, pheasants, and mangel wurzels was carried in on the shoulders of four men. From the middle of the pie a lady appeared, who started the singing of "Auld Lang Syne," and afterwards distributed the hundreds of crackers with which the pie was filled.

FLORAL DECORATIONS.

The floral decorations were in most cases reminiscent of Christmas, with holly, mistletoe, evergreens, and berries predominating. Real flowers, however, were used in many of the restaurants, notably Prince's—where a balloon and an aeroplane made of holly and electrically lit represented the old and the new year respectively, and Tango exhibitions were given in the rose-decorated ballroom—and at the Piccadilly, where the prevailing note in the table decorations was of a soft pink. The menu here, too, was a most artistic piece of work, while the "Welcome, 1914," in lights of many colours was very effective. At the Cecil, the Métropole, the Dieudonné, and the Waldorf, flowers and evergreens were artistically woven into dainty festoons, while the lighting in all cases was arranged to harmonize

The prosecution of war operations obliges me to move my Headquarters away from Berlin. I speak from the bottom of my heart when I bid farewell to the citizens of Berlin and thank them for the demonstrations of love and affection which I have experienced in so rich a measure in these great and fateful days. I have supreme confidence in the help of God, in the bravery of the Army and Navy and in the unbreakable sense of unity of the German people in their hour of peril. Victory will not fail a just cause. Berlin, August 16 1914—Wilhelm IR

1 BRITAIN c1913
Postcard

MY YOUNG MAN'S A SOLDIER,
SIX FOOT HIGH IS HE,
HIS ARM IS STRONG,
HIS WEAPON'S LONG
AND HE'S VERY FOND OF ME.

Donald · McGill.

Der Fortgang der kriegerischen Operationen nötigt Mich, Mein Hauptquartier von Berlin zu verlegen. Es ist Mir ein Herzensbedürfnis, der Berliner Bürgerschaft mit Meinem Lebewohl innigsten Dank zu sagen für alle die Kundgebungen und Beweise der Liebe und Zuneigung, die Ich in diesen großen und schicksalsschweren Tagen in so reichem Maße erfahren habe. Ich vertraue fest auf Gottes Hilfe, auf die Tapferkeit von Heer und Marine und die unerschütterliche Einmütigkeit des deutschen Volkes in den Stunden der Gefahr. Unserer gerechten Sache wird der Sieg nicht fehlen.

Berlin im Schloß, den 16. August 1914.

Wilhelm I. R.

An den Oberbürgermeister von Berlin.

Vorstehenden Erlaß Seiner Majestät des Kaisers bringen wir hiermit zur öffentlichen Kenntnis.

Berlin, den 17. August 1914.

Magistrat der Königlichen Haupt- und Residenzstadt
Wermuth.

2 BERLIN August 1914
Proclamation

The King's Message.

The following is the text of the King's message to his troops delivered before they departed to France:

"You are leaving home to fight for the safety and honour of my Empire. Belgium, whose country we are pledged to defend, has been attacked, and France is about to be invaded by the same powerful foe.

"I have implicit confidence in you, my soldiers. Duty is your watchword, and I know your duty will be nobly done.

"I shall follow your every movement with deepest interest and mark with eager satisfaction your daily progress; indeed, your welfare will never be absent from my thoughts.

"I pray God to bless you and guard you, and bring you back victorious."

3 LONDON August 1914
Press announcement

Bekanntmachung.

Nachdem Seine Majestät der Kaiser und König heute die Mobilmachung der Armee befohlen haben, werden hiermit für den morgigen Sonntag die Bestimmungen bezüglich der Sonntagsruhe außer Kraft gesetzt.

Berlin, den 1. August 1914.

Der Oberbefehlshaber in den Marken.

von Kessel
Generaloberst.

PROCLAMATION Whereas His Majesty the King and Emperor has today ordered the mobilization of the Army, the regulations appointing Sunday as a day of rest are hereby rescinded.—Commander-in-chief, Berlin, August 1 1914

NOTICE TO THE POPULATION In order to assure the security of our troops and calm among the population of Rheims, the persons named have been seized by the Commandant of the German Army as hostages. They will be shot at the slightest disorder. If however the town remains calm and orderly the hostages and the citizens will be placed under the protection of the German Army—General Commander-in-chief, Rheims, September 12 1914

4 BERLIN August 1914   Proclamation

AVIS A LA POPULATION

Afin d'assurer suffisamment la sécurité de nos troupes et le calme de la population de Reims, les personnes nommées ont été saisies comme otages par le Commandant de l'Armée Allemande. Ces otages seront fusillés au moindre **désordre**. D'autre part, si la ville se tient absolument calme et tranquille, ces otages et habitants seront placés sous la protection de l'Armée Allemande.

Le Général Commandant en Chef.

Reims, le 12 Septembre 1914

5 RHEIMS September 1914

AU PEUPLE BELGE

C'est à mon plus grand regret que les troupes allemandes se voient forcées de franchir la frontière de Belgique. Elles agissent sous la contrainte d'une nécessité inévitable. La neutralité de la Belgique ayant été violée par des officiers français qui, sous un déguisement, ont traversé le territoire belge en automobile pour pénétrer en Allemagne.

BELGES !

C'est mon plus grand désir qu'il y ait encore moyen d'éviter un combat entre deux peuples qui étaient amis jusqu'à present, jadis même alliés. Souvenez-vous des glorieux jours de Waterloo où c'étaient les armes allemandes qui ont contribué à fonder et à établir l'indépendance et la prospérité de votre Patrie.

Mais il nous faut le chemin libre. Des destructions de ponts, de tunnels, de voies ferrées, devront être regardées comme des actions hostiles.

BELGES !

Vous avez à choisir ! J'espère que l'armée allemande de la Meuse ne sera pas contrainte de vous combattre. Un chemin libre pour attaquer, c'est tout ce que nous désirons.

Je donne des garanties formelles à la population belge qu'elle n'aura rien à souffrir des horreurs de la guerre, que nous payerons en or-monnaie les vivres qu'il faudra prendre au pays, que nos soldats se montreront les meilleurs amis d'un peuple pour lequel nous éprouvons la plus haute estime, la plus grande sympathie.

C'est de votre sagesse et d'un patriotisme bien compris qu'il dépend d'éviter à votre pays les horreurs de la guerre.

Le Général Commandant en Chef l'Armée de la Meuse,

Von EMMICH

6   BELGIUM August 1914   Proclamation

TO THE BELGIAN PEOPLE It is to my very great regret that German troops find themselves obliged to infringe the Belgian frontier. They act under pressure of unavoidable necessity, Belgium's neutrality having been violated by French officers who, in disguise, have crossed Belgian territory by car to enter Germany. BELGIANS! It is my greatest desire that there still be means of avoiding conflict between two peoples who have been friends up to the present—at one time allies. Remember the glorious days of Waterloo, where it was German arms that contributed to the founding and establishing of the independence and prosperity of your Country. But we must have free access. Destruction of bridges, tunnels, railway tracks, must be regarded as hostile acts. BELGIANS! You have to choose. I hope that the German Army of the Meuse will not be obliged to fight you. A clear road to the attack is all that we desire. I give formal guarantees to the Belgian population that they will not have to suffer the horrors of war, that we will pay in gold currency for provisions which we will need from the country, that our soldiers will show themselves the best friends of a people for whom we hold the highest esteem and the greatest fellow-feeling. On your prudence, no less than on your patriotism, depends your country's avoidance of the horrors of war—General Commander-in-Chief, Army of the Meuse, Von Emmich

---

7   (No hunting if England declares war)

POST OFFICE TELEGRAPHS

Exford

TO { Fox Revenue Hall Taunton

No Hunting if England Declares

War

Tucker (Huntsman)

7   TAUNTON August 1914   Telegram

TO BERLIN!

The Country is arranging a Trip to Germany
in the Spring to a few

SPORTSMEN.

All hotel expenses and railway fares paid.

Good Shooting and Hunting.

Ages 18–38 (?).   Rifles and

AMMUNITION SUPPLIED FREE.

Cheap Trips up the Rhine.

Apply at once as there is only a limited number (one million) required.

APPLY—

PRIVATE DANIEL SHERRIN.
4th Batt. The Buffs,
East Kent Regiment.
Drill Hall,
St. Peter's Lane,
Canterbury.

8   CANTERBURY Sept 1914

---

5 Questions to those who employ male servants

1. **H**AVE you a Butler, Groom, Chauffeur, Gardener, or Gamekeeper serving you who, at this moment should be serving your King and Country?

2. Have you a man serving at your table who should be serving a gun?

3. Have you a man digging your garden who should be digging trenches?

4. Have you a man driving your car who should be driving a transport wagon?

5. Have you a man preserving your game who should be helping to preserve your Country?

A great responsibility rests on you. Will you sacrifice your personal convenience for your Country's need?

Ask your men to enlist **TO-DAY.**

The address of the nearest Recruiting Office can be obtained at any Post Office.

God Save the King.

9   LONDON December 1914   Press ad.

Commandeered

Have any of YOUR Horses or Vans been Commandeered?

We can Supply You with **Motor Vans** on very Reasonable Terms.

The Connaught Motor & Carriage Co., Ltd.,
27-29, Long Acre, London, W.C.

10   LONDON September 1914   Press advertisement

GOUVERNEMENT MILITAIRE DE PARIS

ÉTAT-MAJOR

République Française

ORDRE DE RÉQUISITION DES CHEVAUX

Les chevaux hongres et les juments non requis appartenant aux 9e et 17e arrondissements seront présentés à la Commission de Réquisition n° 16, les 7 et 8 Août courant, à 7 h. 30 du matin.

Le Gouverneur Militaire de Paris,

MICHEL.

ORDER FOR THE REQUISITION OF HORSES
Unrequisitioned geldings and mares belonging to the [9th and 17th] arrondissement will be handed over to Requisition Commission No 16 on August 7 and 8 at 7.30 am.—Military Governor of Paris, Michel.

11   PARIS August 1914   Requisition order

IRON CHRISTMAS is the title of the cover of our Christmas number ['Jugend' magazine] this year. Young Germania, lovelier than ever to behold, and symbol of our nation's honour, decks the good old Christmas tree with coloured lights and Iron Crosses for our dauntless heroes in the field. . . Greetings from home, where a million true hearts beat thankfully for her. . . The Christmas Number will appear on December 24. . . . Available at all bookshops and newsstands. . . .

CITY OF NORWICH.

PUBLIC NOTICE.

THE CITIZENS, in their desire to show their goodwill and hospitality to the Military Forces, have, in some instances, entertained them beyond the bounds of prudence.

I APPEAL THEREFORE to the Citizens that in the best interest of the Nation they will exercise restraint upon their hospitality and friendship.

ANY PERSON desiring to show his appreciation of the valuable services being rendered by our guests may forward to me any amount of money, however small, which shall be devoted to the Soldiers and Sailors' Families Association.

JAMES A. PORTER,

Guildhall, Norwich. LORD MAYOR.
11th August, 1914.

A. E. SOMAN & CO., ST. ANDREW'S PRINTING WORKS, NORWICH.

12 NORWICH August 1914 Public notice

Eiserne Weihnachten

heißt das Titelblatt unserer diesjährigen **Weihnachtsnummer**. Die Jungfer Germania, lieblicher als je anzuschauen, aber in eherner Rüstung, putzt für unsere todesmutigen Helden im Felde den guten alten Kinderbaum mit eisernen Kreuzen und farbigen Lichtlein, Grüßen aus der Heimat, wo Millionen treuer Herzen dankbar für sie schlagen.

Dieses reizende Bild unseres **Julius Diez** und einige andere von unseren Meistern **Angelo Jank** (Generaloberst von Hindenburg), **Erich Wilke** (Der Kapitän der Emden), **Paul Rieth** (Unterm Roten Kreuz), **Julius Diez** (Der Islam rührt sich), **Erich Wilke** (Der Japs im Dienste John Bulls), werden auch in farbiger Verkleinerung als

Ansichts-Postkarten

zur Ausgabe gelangen, welche zum Preise von 10 Pfennig pro Karte etwa anfangs Dezember versandt werden können. Die oben erwähnte Weihnachtsnummer der „Jugend" kommt am 24. Dezember zur Ausgabe und kann zum Preise von 40 Pfennig durch jede Buch- und Kunsthandlung und jedes Zeitungsgeschäft bezogen werden. Gegen Voreinsendung von 80 resp. 50 Pfennig sendet der unterzeichnete Verlag die sechs Ansichts-Postkarten und die Weihnachtsnummer auch direct.

München, Anfang November 1914.
Lessingstraße 1.

Verlag der Münchner „Jugend".

13 MUNICH November 1914 Press announcement

TO OUR READERS In consequence of the burden imposed on our telephone wires we ask that no private telephone requests for information be made at this time. All available important news will be published immediately, either in the normal issues of the 'Frankfurter Zeitung', in extra editions, or through posted bills. The display of important news photographs will continue as previously from 8 o'clock each evening in the Frankfurter Börsenplatz.

14 LEIPZIG 1914 Magazine cover

An unsere Leser!

Wegen Ueberlastung unserer Telephonleitungen bitten wir, in dieser Zeit von uns keine privaten telephonischen Auskünfte zu verlangen. Alle eingehenden wichtigen Nachrichten werden sofort durch Anschlag, durch Extrablätter sowie durch die regelmäßigen Ausgaben der „Frankfurter Zeitung" veröffentlicht. Von abends 8 Uhr ab erfolgt wie bisher die Bekanntgabe aller wichtigen Nachrichten durch Lichtbild am Frankfurter Börsenplatz.

15 FRANKFURT August 1914 Press announcement

Chief Constable's Office,
Taunton, 17th August, 1914.

To Supt. Division.

In order to avoid any interference whatever with recruiting for the Army of 100,000 men called for by Lord Kitchener please see that likely men for this new Army are not employed as volunteer guards.

The conditions of age for such enlistment are as follows:—

For untrained men from 19 to 30.

For ex-soldiers up to 42.

Please send a copy of this memorandum to the various gentlemen in your Division who are undertaking the raising &c., of the various sections of volunteers, for their information and guidance.

Also a copy of the Railway Regulations attached.

H.C. METCALFE Captain.
Chief Constable.

16 TAUNTON August 1914 Circular

SELFRIDGE'S

FOR the convenience of Visitors and Customers several features have been provided which cannot fail to be of general interest during the War. There are several "War Windows," the chief of which contains a large Flagged War Map, showing the trend of events. Others exhibit War News Bulletins & War Photographs

DESPITE the unsettled state of affairs, the business now being transacted in this House is almost normal. The quality of our merchandise is unaltered by external events: it can be depended on always and absolutely. Where the non-arrival of Continental merchandise is likely to cause a difficulty, our stocks are, wherever possible, being filled with British-Made goods of the highest quality. Our prices are still, as always—Quality for Quality—"London's lowest."

To those Visitors who are in London at the present time, and may have, perhaps, lost their Luggage, we submit the following list. It is intended to be suggestive only.

Light Suit Cases, Cabin Trunks, Carry-Alls. Steamer Coats in the new Civet Cat and Leopard Plush. Pyjamas, Hand-embroidered Underwear and Woven Underwear of almost every style and weave, Felt and Velvet Hats for Town and Steamer wear, Steamer Rugs in Scotch Plaid and reverse plain colours, Camel Hair Rugs, Navy Blue Steamer Frocks, Travelling Suits, Umbrellas, Stockings, Boots and Shoes.

SCIENTIFIC & ELECTRICAL EXHIBITION

To be held in the Palm Court from To-day until August 29th. The exhibits include some of the most interesting of modern inventions. There will also be an Exhibition of Gladioli by Messrs. Kelway, of Langport, Somerset, in the Palm Court, from Tues. to Fri. Admission to both Exhibitions is, of course, quite free

TO ALL SAILORS AND SOLDIERS,

Territorials, Regulars, or Volunteers called upon for service we will present free Three Copies of their Photograph in Uniform. Studio on the First Floor of the new Men's Store, Marble Arch end of our Island Site.

A RED CROSS DEPOT

has been opened on the Ground Floor to supply Everything required by Ladies working for the British Red Cross Society or Nursing Associations. Purchasers of material will be supplied free with copies of the official garment-patterns. Every assistance will gladly be given to ladies organising Nursing Corps or equipping Private Hospitals.

TO THE LADY who is prepared to help her country by making Garments, etc., for the Soldier and Sailor on Active Service, our large and varied assortment of the following suitable materials will appeal:

FLANNELS (White, Natural, Grey, and Red,) for Bed Jackets, Day or Night Shirts.

UNBLEACHED CALICO for Bandages.

Special Hospital UNBLEACHED TWILL for Night Shirts.

WHITE TWILL CALICO for Night Shirts.

THE "TRIPLE COMFORTER," a combined Sleeping Cap, Cholera Belt, and Muffler. The necessary Wool, Knitting Needles, or Crochet Hooks obtainable here.

This garment is easily made, and FREE LESSONS are given daily in the Art Needlework Dept. (1st Floor).

SPECIALITY Khaki - coloured Wool for making and mending Cardigan Jackets and other garments.

GIFT OF BANKNOTE COVERS

A neat case to take the new Paper Currency presented free. To be obtained in the Stationery Dept.—Ground Floor.

PETROL !

1st quality A gallon **1/8**
2nd quality A gallon **1/6**

Cars must be filled here. We cannot deliver Petrol.

War Maps and Flags at all prices in the Book Dept., Ground Floor.

RIFLE PRACTICE ON THE ROOF

Our sub-target on the roof is, as usual, without charge, at the disposal of all visitors. The target automatically records the "hits" made. A qualified attendant is in charge, and will give instruction and advice free.

SELFRIDGE & CO., LTD., OXFORD ST., W.

FOR MEMBERS of His Majesty's Forces, Nurses, and Others, at present serving their country—

Officer's Folding Waterproof Canvas VALISE and Sleeping-Bag.

For the Motor Cyclist—Waterproof Motor-Cycling JACKET and OVER-ALLS.

Fleece SLEEPING BAG (when rolled up occupies quite small space).

Also Waterproof GROUND-SHEET, indispensable for the Motorist on active service.

NURSE'S UNIFORM DRESS (Nursecloth).

Cotton Washing WALLET, for fastening on belt.

RED CROSS APRONS, ARMY CAPS.

OVERALLS for Nurses and others, in Butcher and White, and Navy and White Stripes.

FIRST-AID CASES. Rubber Bed Sheets, Lint, Cotton Wool Bandages, Hygienic Sponges, &c.

Red Cross Nurse's Khaki Rubber RAINCOAT and HAT to roll up into small haversack of the same material.

22 SARTHE, FRANCE
September 1914
Special news bulletin

L'INFORMATEUR (Special news sheet): *PROCLAMATION* The Government addresses the following proclamation to the country: Frenchmen . . . for several weeks our heroic troops and the army of the enemy have been engaged in fierce fighting. The valour of our soldiers has afforded them marked advantages at several points, but in the north the thrust of the German forces has obliged us to retire.

This situation imposes a painful decision on the President of the Republic and the Government. As guardians of the safety of the state, the public authorities have the duty to withdraw, for the moment, from the City of Paris.

Under the direction of a distinguished commander, a French army—an army of courage and spirit—will defend the capital and its patriotic inhabitants against the invader. But the war must be prosecuted at the same time in the rest of the country. Without pause or respite, without fail or falter, the sacred struggle for the honour of the nation and for the reparation of violated rights will continue.

Not one of our armies is impaired. If some among them have suffered noticeable losses, the gaps have immediately been filled and the call for replacements assures us of new resources and new strength for tomorrow.

Stand and fight—this must be the password for the allied armies—English, Russian, Belgian and French. Stand and fight, while on the sea the English help us to cut off the enemy's communication with the outside world. Stand and fight, while the Russians continue their advance, bringing a decisive blow at the heart of the German Empire. It is for the Government of the Republic to direct this stubborn defence. . . . At the request of the military authority the Government transfers its seat to a location from which it will be able to maintain close contact with the whole of the country. . . . The Government leaves Paris only after having assured the defence of the city and garrison. . . . It knows that it need not enjoin the worthy people of Paris to calm, to resolution and to confidence. They show, day by day, that they are a match for the greatest of French duties. Let us all be worthy of these tragic circumstances. Ours will be the final victory. It will be ours by unflagging will, by endurance and by tenacity. A nation which will not perish, and which, to live, retreats neither before suffering nor before sacrifice, is assured of victory—President of the French Republic, R Poincaré

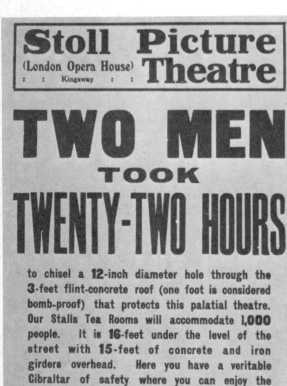

21 LONDON c1915 Poster

10ᵉ Année. — N° 61   Première Édition   Jeudi 3 Septembre 1914

L'INFORMATEUR
5 centimes   5 centimes

DE LA SARTHE

PROCLAMATION

Le Gouvernement adresse au Pays la proclamation suivante :

FRANÇAIS,

Depuis plusieurs semaines, des combats acharnés mettent aux prises nos troupes héroïques et l'armée ennemie. La vaillance de nos soldats leur a valu, sur plusieurs points, des avantages marqués; mais, au Nord, la poussée des forces Allemandes nous a contraints à nous replier.

Cette situation impose au Président de la République et au Gouvernement une décision douloureuse. Pour veiller au salut National, les pouvoirs publics ont le devoir de s'éloigner, pour l'instant, de la Ville de Paris.

Sous le commandement d'un chef éminent une armée française pleine de courage et d'entrain défendra contre l'envahisseur la Capitale et sa patriotique population. Mais la guerre doit se poursuivre en même temps sur le reste du territoire. Sans paix ni trêve, sans arrêt ni défaillance, continuera la lutte sacrée pour l'honneur de la Nation, et pour la réparation du droit violé.

Aucune de nos armées n'est entamée. Si quelques-unes d'entre elles ont subi des pertes trop sensibles, les vides ont été immédiatement comblés par le dépôt et l'appel des recrues assure pour demain de nouvelles ressources en hommes et en énergies.

Durer et combattre, tel doit être le mot d'ordre des armées alliées : Anglaise, Russe, Belge et Française. Durer et combattre pendant que sur mer les anglais nous aident à couper les communications de notre ennemi avec le monde. Durer et combattre pendant que les Russes continuent à s'avancer pour porter au cœur de l'empire d'Allemagne le coup décisif. C'est au Gouvernement de la République qu'il appartient de diriger cette résistance opiniâtre. Partout pour l'indépendance, les Français se lèveront pour donner à cette lutte formidable tout son élan et toute son efficacité. Il reste indispensable que le Gouvernement demeure libre d'agir. A la demande de l'autorité militaire, le Gouvernement

L'INFORMATEUR

transporte donc momentanément sa résidence sur un point du territoire d'où il puisse rester en relations constantes avec l'ensemble du pays. Il invite les Membres du Parlement à ne pas se tenir éloignés de lui pour pouvoir former devant l'ennemi avec le Gouvernement et leurs collègues le faisceau de l'unité nationale.

Le Gouvernement ne quitte Paris qu'après avoir assuré la défense de la Ville et du Camp retranché par tous les moyens en son pouvoir. Il sait qu'il n'a pas besoin de recommander à l'admirable population parisienne le calme, la résolution et le sang-froid. Elle montre, tous les jours, qu'elle est à la hauteur des plus grands devoirs Français. Soyons tous dignes de ces tragiques circonstances. Nous obtiendrons la Victoire finale. Nous l'obtiendrons par la volonté inlassable, par l'endurance et par la ténacité. Une Nation qui ne veut pas périr et qui, pour vivre, ne recule ni devant la souffrance, ni devant le sacrifice, est sûre de vaincre.

Signé :

Le Président de la République Française,
R. POINCARÉ.

Le Président du Conseil des Ministres,
René VIVIANI.

La Situation Générale

A notre aile gauche dans la journée du 1ᵉʳ Septembre, un corps de cavalerie allemande dans sa marche dans la forêt de Compiègne a eu un engagement avec les Anglais qui lui ont

GRAND ASSAULT
ON
GERMANY'S TRADE

Every Unit of Commerce to Stand by the Government

ROYAL WORCESTER CORSETS
TO THE FRONT.

The Government's Declaration of War upon Germany's trade is a Master-stroke. It arouses the old fighting spirit in every Briton. It outweighs a thousand times the appeals for calmness and steady trade issued by those West End houses who owe their very existence as well as their prosperity to Britain, and yet pay their debt by sending their corset orders to GERMANY, or other Continental manufacturing centres! These German corsets are offered to the public as the drapers' Specialities, or are cunningly disguised under some fancy name or initials. We imagine, too, that it would astonish many of our patriotic drapers if they knew what huge quantities of German corsets are exported to Paris and afterwards shipped to this country as French corsets.

"WAR UPON GERMANY'S TRADE!"—The Government's Declaration calls upon every Corset-Maker for active service in the War upon Germany's trade.

Ladies must—and will—have corsets. Drapers *must* sell them. But the closing of the Continental markets has cut off the sources of supply to those drapers who have knowingly pushed German corsets, or unknowingly pushed so-called French corsets made in Germany. A deluge of new business from these sources is now to be won. But unfortunately many Corset-Makers here at home are unable to take advantage of this golden opportunity because they have always bought their busks and steels from Germany and can no longer get supplies. Consequently several are already working short-handed, and one large factory has closed down altogether. We ourselves buy nothing from Germany, and for a long time past have used only the best Lancashire and French coutils. Having large stocks of raw materials and huge contracts, we can hold out longer than other houses, and by almost superhuman efforts we are managing to cope with the flood of new business that is reaching us. An occasion like this, however, binds us all together, and we shall be only too happy to supply any other corset manufacturers with busks and steels, and to render them every assistance possible in order that they may keep their factories going during the War, and to enable them to *come into the fighting line and capture Germany's trade!*

The principals and every employé of the Royal Worcester Warehouse Co. are British-born, and the concern is run entirely upon British capital. A number of members of the Staff have gone to the front, and will be paid during their absence, their places being held open for them till they return.

The Worcester Building,
(FOR ROYAL WORCESTER CORSETS),
103-78, Mortimer St., London, W. (Wholesale).

23   LONDON 1914   Press advertisement

Mothers!

Have you forgotten the Belgian Atrocities?
Do you realise what will be the lot of you and your children if the Germans successfully invade England?
The "Lusitania" Massacre should convince you of the length to which Germany is prepared to go in her policy of "frightfulness."
Do you expect other Mothers' sons to defend **you and your sons**?
Persuade your son to enlist—do not hold him back.
One word from **YOU** and he will go.

Sweethearts!

Has your "boy" enlisted?
If not, why not?
Are you selfishly dissuading him?
If so the shame of your Country rests upon **YOU**.
If you cannot persuade him to answer his Country's Call and protect you now

Discharge him
as unfit!

Enlist at the nearest Recruiting Office.

God Save the King!

24   LONDON 1915   Leaflet

25   LONDON 1915
Window disk

The death penalty is imposed on all acts of hostility directed against the Establishment of the German army, also against the removal, damaging or impairment of arms, articles of equipment, etc, etc. . . . or of buildings or institutions of any sort which the German Army holds for its use. . . . In each area hostages from various classes of the population will be answerable with their lives for the lawfulness of acts of the communities from which they are drawn.

BEKANNTMACHUNG.

Jede feindselige Handlung gegen alle Angehörigen des deutschen Heeres, jede Wegnahme, Beschädigung oder Vernichtung von Waffen, Ausrüstungsstücken, Heeresgeräten, Vorräten und Materialien aller Art und die Beschädigung aller Verkehrs-Anlagen, insbesondere Strassen, Brücken, Eisenbahnen, Telegrafen- und Telefonleitungen, sowie aller sonstigen vom deutschen Heere in Benutzung genommenen Gebäude und Einrichtungen

wird mit dem Tode bestraft.

Die gleiche Strafe trifft den, der eine solche Tat versucht, dazu auffordert, Hilfe leistet oder von ihr Kenntnis hat und nicht sofort Anzeige erstattet.

Als Geiseln werden in jedem Orte aus allen Bevölkerungsschichten eine Anzahl Personen in Haft genommen, die mit ihrem Leben dafür haften, dass die Bevölkerung sich jeder feindseligen Handlung enthält.

. . . . . . den . . . . . .

BEKENDMAKING.

Iedere vijandelijke handeling tegen allen leden van het Duitsch leger, elke ontvreemding, beschadiging of vernieling van wapens, stukken der uitrusting, legergereedschappen, voorraden, voorwerpen en materialen van allen soorten, en de beschadiging van allen verkeersinrichtingen, vooral straten, bruggen, spoorwegen, leidingen voor telegraaf en telefoon, alsmede van allen andere gebouwen en inrichtingen, welke van het Duitsch leger in gebruik genomen zijn.

wordt met den dood gestraft.

Dezelfde straf moet diegene ondergaan, welke eene dergelijke daad beproeft uit te voeren, hiertoe opstookt, helpt of kennis ervan heeft en niet onmiddellijk aangifte doet.

Van iedere plaats worden een getal personen van elken rang en stand als gijzelaars in hechtenis genomen. Zij staan met hun leven daarvoor in, dat de bevolking zich van iedere vijandelijke handeling onthoudt.

ORDRE.

La peine de mort

est comminée contre tout acte d'hostilité dirigé contre les ressortissants de l'armée allemande, contre également tous enlèvement, endommagement ou détérioration d'armes, objets d'équipement, ustensiles, stocks ou enfin matériaux de tous genres à l'usage ou à la disposition de l'armée allemande, ou encore contre l'endommagement de tous les trafics organisés, notamment les routes, ponts, chemins de fer, fils téléphoniques ou télégraphiques ou enfin tous les bâtiments ou institutions quelconques que l'armée allemande tient sous usage.

La même peine de mort est comminée contre toute tentative ayant pour objet d'amener l'exécution d'un des actes prohibés énoncés ci-dessus ainsi que contre le fait de prêter assistance à l'un de ces actes ou contre le fait cette d'avoir connaissance de l'un de ces actes ou tentatives sans les dénoncer immédiatement.

Dans chaque agglomération, des ôtages, choisis dans les différentes classes de la population, répondront sur leur vie de la licité des agissements de la population du sein de laquelle ils auront été tirés.

26   BELGIUM 1914   Proclamation

Educated Women as War Workers.

A PRACTICAL SCHEME.

Work commenced on July 19th, 1915.

It is daily becoming more evident that the nation must make use to the utmost extent of all its powers of productivity if it is to emerge triumphant from the greatest War which it has ever waged. The working women at present employed in munition factories are already fully engaged in producing the largest possible "output" from the machinery available which is running on eight-hour shifts seven days and seven nights a week. In order that these willing workers may not be over-taxed, it is important to relieve them of overtime, especially of Sunday labour, for only thus can their efficiency be fully maintained over a prolonged period.

A scheme has therefore been devised to ensure the week-end rest for these factory hands by training educated women of the leisured class not over 50 years of age in munition factories, and for forming out of this specially trained band of workers a relieving body who will take Saturday and Sunday overtime work, thus enabling the ordinary wage-earner to get the rest necessary to sustain her efficiency and productivity at its highest point.

Arrangements have been made with Messrs. Vickers to train at Erith the first of these volunteer bands of educated women to enable them to replace, to the extent indicated above, the working women at the machines in the various departments of the manufacture of shells. These volunteers, after three weeks' training, will undertake regular week-end relief work, and so serve the double purpose of helping to keep the factory hands efficient, without competing against them, and providing for the much-needed Saturday and Sunday "off" while at the same time maintaining the output of ammunition essential to victory. As the first step towards the realisation of this scheme, a large house has been taken at Erith, and has been furnished and fitted up as a hostel, with accommodation for about 30 ladies.

In every case a personal interview is desirable.

27   LONDON 1915   Leaflet

D. O. R. A.

REGULATION 40 D.

No woman who is suffering from venereal disease in a communicable form shall have sexual intercourse with any member of His Majesty's forces or solicit or invite any member of His Majesty's forces to have sexual intercourse with her.

If a woman acts in contravention of this regulation she shall be guilty of a summary offence against these regulations.

A woman charged with an offence under this regulation shall if she so requires be remanded for a period (not less than a week) for the purpose of such medical examination as may be requisite for ascertaining whether she is suffering from such a disease as aforesaid.

The defendant shall be informed of her right to be remanded as aforesaid and that she may be examined by her own Doctor or by the Medical Officer of the Prison.

In this regulation the expression "venereal disease" means syphilis, gonorrhœa, or soft chancre.

THIS is a first step in the direction of State Regulation of Vice. It is an attempt to introduce **Compulsory Medical Examination** of prostitutes under another guise. Why is a woman to be "informed of her *right*" to examination if not because she is to be forced, when charged, to establish her innocence—if she is able—by this means?

The object of the regulation is to "protect" soldiers from disease. They need never run into danger of venereal disease. They have the alternative of clean living, and it is an insult to them to assume that they leave behind them in France the courage which enables them to face the horrors of war, so that on their return they are too cowardly to say "No" to an importunate prostitute. Are they to be "protected" from a risk which they need never run at the expense of the women whose awful calling is the result of men's demand for it?

But, in any case, it is not possible to make vice "safe" by these means. The highest authorities on prostitution in Europe are agreed that the **medical examination of Prostitutes does not check the spread of venereal disease.** On the contrary, it too often leads to a false sense of security amongst men which actually increases the danger. This regulation will make the streets *less* "safe" for our soldiers.

Lastly, do the soldiers themselves want this sort of "protection," even if it could be effective? They go abroad to fight for their country and their womankind—are they willing to have women persecuted so that on their return they may indulge their vices the more freely? Is it not an insult to suggest such a thing?

There is a better way to "protect" them—with knowledge. How many would lead cleaner lives if they were made to understand, not only the dangers they were running and the risk to an innocent wife and children, but also the spiritual degradation both to themselves and to the women with whom they consort. Our soldiers, many of them mere boys, are led astray through their ignorance. They need, not outside "protection," but to be taught to protect themselves by self-control.

Printed by C. F. Hodgson & Son, Newton Street, W.C.2, and published by the Independent Women's Social and Political Union, 5 Duke Street, Adelphi.

28   LONDON 1915   Leaflet

THE PHARMACIE NORMALE informs its customers that it will remain open every day until 7 o'clock—Sundays excepted—but as a result of the departure of very large numbers of employees to join the colours, it will be unable to undertake home deliveries.

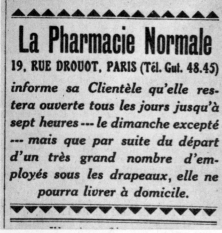

La Pharmacie Normale

19, RUE DROUOT, PARIS (Tél. Gut. 48.45)

informe sa Clientèle qu'elle restera ouverte tous les jours jusqu'à sept heures --- le dimanche excepté --- mais que par suite du départ d'un très grand nombre d'employés sous les drapeaux, elle ne pourra livrer à domicile.

29   PARIS 1914   Press announcement

Truppen Frankfurt a. M., Neue Mainzerstr. 58 pt.

NOTICE.

The Railroad authorities have agreed to place a train at the service of the American citizens now in Frankfurt, to go to Rotterdam on Friday, August 21, provided that at least 300 persons will avail themselves of the opportunity.

In order to secure this train, the authorities must be notified before 3 P.M. Wednesday, August 19, and persons who wish to travel by this train, must sign an agreement, pledging themselves to that effect, at the office of the American Consul-General, before 1 P.M. Wednesday, August 19.

Places will be reserved **only** for persons who sign this agreement. Baggage will be taken.

Tickets: 1. class ...... M. 38.—
2. ,, ... ,, 25.—

Signors of similar previous lists or petitions for special train are hereby notified that they **must sign** the new agreement, in order to have the privilege to participate in the use of the special train.

Notice of time of departure of train, if provided, will be given later.   D38655

Preußische Central-Bodenkredit-

30   PARIS 1914   Press announcement

NO TREATING

Under the Defence of the Realm Act Every person must pay for their own drink at the time of ordering.

31   LONDON 1915   Notice

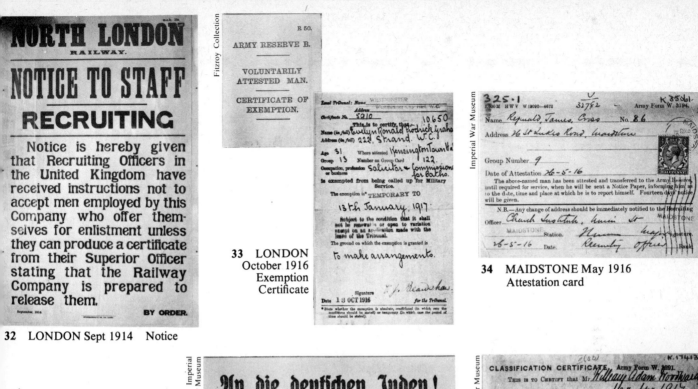

NORTH LONDON RAILWAY.

NOTICE TO STAFF

RECRUITING

Notice is hereby given that Recruiting Officers in the United Kingdom have received instructions not to accept men employed by this Company who offer themselves for enlistment unless they can produce a certificate from their Superior Officer stating that the Railway Company is prepared to release them.

BY ORDER.

32 LONDON Sept 1914 Notice

R 50.

ARMY RESERVE B.

VOLUNTARILY ATTESTED MAN.

CERTIFICATE OF EXEMPTION.

33 LONDON October 1916 Exemption Certificate

34 MAIDSTONE May 1916 Attestation card

Un die deutschen Juden!

TO GERMAN JEWS In fateful hours, the Fatherland calls its sons to the colours. That every German Jew is ready as duty demands for sacrifice of life and wealth goes without saying. Fellow believers! We call upon you to give your all—to dedicate your whole strength to the Fatherland. Hasten to the flag! All—men and women—place yourselves at the service of the Fatherland . . . in personal relief work of all descriptions, and in the giving of cash and kind.—Society of German Jews; Central Union of German-Citizen Jewish Believers.

35 BERLIN August 1914   Press announcement

CLASSIFICATION CERTIFICATE

36 LONDON April 1917 Classification certificate

For the War.

1914— League of Honour.

For Women and Girls of the Empire.

Motto: "Strength and Honour."

Member's Promise: "I promise, by the help of God, to do all that is in my power to uphold the honour of our Empire and its defenders in this time of war, by Prayer, Purity, and Temperance."

Member's Signature _____

Enrolling Officer _____

Temperance War Pledge: "I promise, by the help of God, to abstain from all Alcoholic Drinks, as beverages, during the war, and to encourage others to do the same."

Member's Signature _____

Enrolling Officer _____

37 LONDON 1914   Pledge certificate

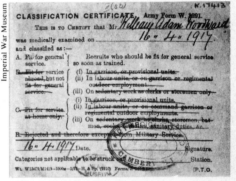

[This paper is to be considered by each soldier as confidential, and to be kept in his Active Service Pay Book.]

You are ordered abroad as a soldier of the King to help our French comrades against the invasion of a common Enemy. You have to perform a task which will need your courage, your energy, your patience. Remember that the honour of the British Army depends on your individual conduct. It will be your duty not only to set an example of discipline and perfect steadiness under fire but also to maintain the most friendly relations with those whom you are helping in this struggle. The operations in which you are engaged will, for the most part, take place in a friendly country, and you can do your own country no better service than in showing yourself in France and Belgium in the true character of a British soldier.

Be invariably courteous, considerate and kind. Never do anything likely to injure or destroy property,

and always look upon looting as a disgraceful act. You are sure to meet with a welcome and to be trusted; your conduct must justify that welcome and that trust. Your duty cannot be done unless your health is sound. So keep constantly on your guard against any excesses. In this new experience you may find temptations both in wine and women. You must entirely resist both temptations, and, while treating all women with perfect courtesy, you should avoid any intimacy.

Do your duty bravely.

Fear God.

Honour the King.

KITCHENER,
Field-Marshal.

38 LONDON November 1914   Leaflet

NORTH EASTERN RAILWAY.

WITHDRAWAL OF RESTAURANT CARS.

On and from 1st MAY, 1916,

the whole of the Dining, Restaurant etc. Cars, running over the North Eastern Railway (including those on the East Coast Trains between London, King's Cross, and Scotland) will be discontinued except on the

8-55 a.m. LEEDS to GLASGOW,

5-0 p.m. GLASGOW (6-25 p.m. from Edinburgh) to LEEDS,

12-40 p.m. YORK to NEWCASTLE.

The Breakfast Car on the 8-0 a.m. from Newcastle will not run beyond York.

The following alterations will also be made :—

A Tea and Dining Car will be attached to the 4-50 p.m. Newcastle to York, and will be transferred to the 6-34 p.m York to Doncaster.

A Dining and Supper Car will be attached at Doncaster to the 5 30 p.m from King's Cross to Newcastle, which will be due to leave Doncaster at 8-30 p.m.

York, 20th April, 1916.

Ben Johnson & Co., Ltd., York.

39 YORK April 1916 Leaflet

HEADQUARTERS, No. 2 DISTRICT,
HAMILTON, N.B., JANUARY 30TH, 1915.

My Lord

DEAR SIR,—

As you are probably aware, we have certain information that Enemy Aircraft are working constantly in the South of Scotland, and especially in the Counties of Dumfries, Kirkcudbright, Ayr and Wigtown, in one of which counties a base for supplies, etc., is believed to exist.

It is probable that one of the Planes is a Hydroplane, so that its base must lie either in some sheltered part of the coast line or in one of the numerous lochs existing in the above-mentioned counties.

Owing to the difficulties of supply, transport, etc., and unfavourable climatic conditions, it is obviously impracticable that any protracted operations by His Majesty's Troops can take place in the mountainous districts at this time of year, and **I therefore venture to ask your aid in tracing the suspected base and in tracking down any foreign or disloyal persons who may be in league with the enemy.**

My suggestion is that you instruct your Gamekeepers, Farmers, Shepherds, or other reliable employees to thoroughly search, and, so far as is possible, to watch, all lochs, caves, woods, or other possible hiding places on your estate, and to immediately report any suspicious circumstance that may come to their notice.

Also, to observe and locate any Signalling, either by Flash Light or by means of Interchangeable Coloured Lamps (usually worked by wires on tree tops), and, if possible, to discover the Operators.

I would further suggest that, in order to give authority, one of your most reliable men should be sworn in as a Special Constable.

An immediate Report of any suspicious circumstances should be made to me. Telephone No. **299,** Hamilton; Telegraphic Address, **"Group,"** Hamilton.

I desire to express my sincere thanks to all those who have already assisted me in this most difficult work, and I confidently rely on their further aid in defeating the object of the enemy and ensuring the safety of the Kingdom.

Yours faithfully,

STANLEY PATERSON, COLONEL,
Commanding No. 2 District.

40 HAMILTON, SCOTLAND January 1916 Circular

41 BRITAIN 1915-18 Charity flag

---

278   CHAPTER XI.

The employment of an offensive flank when working over open ground has small chance of success against an enemy with any capacity for manœuvre. On the other hand, in working over ground screened from view and fire an offensive flank, if skilfully led, often promises important advantages which justify its employment.

7. When, owing to the proximity of the enemy, there is not sufficient space to form to the front for attack, the force may be moved to a flank in such a manner that, when the moment for the delivery of the attack arrives and the troops are wheeled in the direction of the enemy, it will be in attack formation. This method of attack may also be used for deceiving the enemy as to the true direction in which the final attack will be delivered.

204. *Final deployment and charge.*

1. Careful observation of the enemy, and accurate calculation of space and time are necessary to ensure that the attack is delivered at the right moment.

2. The several lines must retain their power of changing direction as long as possible. The second and third lines may often be able to retain this power longer than the first line, as they may not have a definite objective in front of them when the attack is first launched.

3. The intervals between units are not required in the attack; regimental and squadron leaders should, therefore, close their regiments and squadrons in on the directing unit as soon as the final deployment is commenced.

4. Movements should be rapid but without haste or confusion, and complicated manœuvres and long words of command should be avoided.

5. In order to economise energy and retain cohesion for the shock, the attacking troops will remain as long as possible at the trot; they will increase the pace to a gallop in sufficient time to permit of the charge being made with the necessary momentum,

MOUNTED ACTION.   279

but cohesion must not be sacrificed for pace. Should an opportunity occur of surprising the enemy, or of striking him before or during deployment, the gallop may be commenced at a considerable distance from the objective.

6. When the commander wishes to obtain the necessary momentum in anticipation of the charge (usually at about 300 to 500 yards distance from the enemy) he will give the command "LINE WILL ATTACK." The pace will then be slightly increased, swords and lances will be brought to the engage; every horse must be thoroughly in hand, the men must be riding close, and there should be two distinct and well-defined ranks; troop leaders will be careful to keep their correct distance from the directing troop leader, and on no account should they exceed this distance; flank guides will press in towards the centre of their troops; and the rear rank men will fill up any gaps which may occur in the rank in front of them.

Just prior to the charge being ordered the regimental and squadron commanders should be on, or approximately on, the same alignment as the troop leaders.

7. By his skill in choosing the right moment for the charge the leader can increase his chance of success. The shorter the distance over which the charge is made, the greater will be the cohesion and the fresher will be the horses for the actual shock.

The charge should not be ordered, therefore, until the line is about 50 yards distant from the enemy.

8. On the command "CHARGE" one cheer will be given, the front rank will bring swords to the sword in line, and every man will tighten his grip of the saddle and increase his speed with the fixed determination of riding the enemy down.

9. After the charge, the situation may develop in one of three ways :—

(i) The enemy may not meet the attack, but turn about before the collision and retreat.

42 BRITAIN 1916 Field Service Regulations

Dense lines of skirmishers standing, suffer heavy losses at ranges of 1,650 yards (1,500 m.) and under. At lines of skirmishers lying, good effect is to be expected at 1,100 yards (1,000 m.) and under, provided that the observation of fire is good.

582. Against *artillery in action*, the fire effect is similar to that of infantry. Owing to the mobility of machine gun batteries they are especially adapted for securing the increased fire effect due to oblique fire.

583. At short ranges under hostile fire, machine guns can only be brought up and withdrawn under cover.

584. Machine guns, even when on their wheeled carriages, are able to emit a large volume of well-aimed fire in a short space of time.

CAVALRY.

585. The result of *a cavalry charge* depends upon the boldness with which it is led, the selection of the opportune moment, the keenness of the men, the condition of the horses, and the strength and formation of the force employed.

586. Against cavalry, everything depends on the vigour and concentration of the shock. The chance of success is much increased when it is possible to catch the enemy's cavalry in the act of deploying. Envelopment enhances the effect of the charge. Amid the swaying mass of horsemen, the last formed body of cavalry flung into the struggle may decide the result.

587. Against *unshaken infantry*, a cavalry charge has only a prospect of success if delivered completely by surprise. If the cavalry is obliged to charge, it must do so in deep formation and in unity of action, and the charge must be obstinately driven home. A simultaneous charge from different sides may result favourably.

Against *shaken infantry*, cavalry charges will often be successful. It is not then absolutely necessary to charge in deep formation.

588. The principles for charging infantry apply equally against *machine guns* in action.

589. *Artillery*, attacked on the move, and unable to bring its guns into action, is helpless, unless it can make use of carbine or rifle fire. Artillery in action is most vulnerable on the unsupported flank. A frontal attack against artillery will only succeed under exceptionally favourable circumstances; here, again, it is best to charge in deep formation. A charge against artillery will only be completely successful, when the guns and limbers have been carried off or rendered useless.

590. Under infantry fire at short and medium ranges, cavalry can only manœuvre with heavy loss. Heavy losses within the zone of fire effect of hostile artillery can only be avoided by rapidity of movement.

591. Almost as much attention is to be given to

Fitzroy Collection

Be silent! Be wary! Enemy ears are listening.

TAISEZ=VOUS!
MÉFIEZ - VOUS !
Les oreilles ennemies
vous écoutent

44 FRANCE November 1915 Notice

Imperial War Museum

PUZZLE : FIND THE GERMAN SPY.

45 BRITAIN 1914 Postcard translucency

We Germans fear God
—naught else in the world.

46 GERMANY 1915
New Year card

The Lord helps those who help
themselves. Let us subscribe to the
National Loan. Let us contribute to
victory and hasten peace.

47 ITALY c1916 Illustration

POLICE NOTICE.

DEFENCE OF THE REALM ACT, 1914.

ORDER AS TO LIGHTS IN THE CITY OF BIRMINGHAM.

THE FOLLOWING ORDER HAS BEEN ISSUED BY THE SECRETARY OF STATE FOR THE HOME DEPARTMENT:—

"In pursuance of the power conferred on me by Regulation 7A of the Defence of the Realm Regulations, I hereby make the following Order in regard to Lights in the City of Birmingham :—

1. All sky signs and conspicuous illuminated lettering, and powerful external lights used for advertising or the illumination of shop fronts, shall be extinguished.

2. In brightly-lighted streets and squares a portion of the powerful lights shall be extinguished or lowered, and ALL lights which are not extinguished shall be shaded or obscured so as to cut off direct light from the lamp in all directions above the horizontal.

3. All large lighted roof areas shall be covered over or obscured, or the lighting intensity reduced to the minimum possible.

4. The lights of tramcars and omnibuses must not be more than is sufficient to enable fares to be collected."

All Persons concerned will kindly take Notice of this Order.

The Secretary of State further directs that preparation should be made so that more general reduction of lighting could be enforced, on the lines at present adopted in London, and that steps may be taken to this end.

The Regulations referred to are given below. They are not in force at present save so far as they are contained in the above Order. Should the Admiralty so advise they may be put in force at any time, and all Owners of Premises in the City are advised to take Notice of the Provisions.

ORDER AS TO LIGHTS IN LONDON.

(1) In all brightly-lighted streets and squares and on bridges, a portion of the lights must be extinguished so as to break up all conspicuous groups or rows of lights ; and the lights which are not so extinguished must be lowered or made invisible from above by shading them, or by painting over the tops and upper portions of the globes ; provided that while thick fog prevails the lighting of the streets may be resumed.

(3) The intensity of the inside lighting of shop fronts must be reduced from 6 p.m., or earlier if the Commissioner of Police on any occasion so directs.

(4) In tall buildings which are illuminated at night, the greater part of the windows must be shrouded, but lights of moderate brightness may be left uncovered at irregular intervals.

(6) The lighting of railway stations, sidings, and goods yards must be reduced to the intensity sufficient for the safe conduct of business there. The upper half of the globes of all arc lights must be shaded or painted over.

(9) The use of powerful lamps on motor or other vehicles is prohibited.

(10) The aggregation of flares in street markets or elsewhere is prohibited.

(11) In case of sudden emergency, all instructions given by the Admiralty, or by the Commissioner of Police on the advice of the Admiralty, as to the further reduction or extinction of lights shall be immediately obeyed.

This Order shall apply to the City of London and the whole of the Metropolitan Police District, and, except where otherwise provided, to the hours between sunset and sunrise, and it shall be in force for two months from this date unless sooner revoked.

Nos. 2, 5, 7, and 8 of the London Order are omitted as they are covered by the Home Office Order given above, applicable to Birmingham.

CHARLES HAUGHTON RAFTER,
Chief Constable.

23rd November, 1914, Birmingham.

(7135)   PERCIVAL JONES LIMITED, 148-149, GREAT CHARLES STREET, BIRMIEGHAM.

48 BIRMINGHAM November 1914 Police notice

49   NEW YORK May 1915

50   NEW YORK 1915   Poster

1   NEW YORK December 1916   Postal cover

1942

Kommunalverbar

Nicht
übertragbar.

Brotk

Die Gewichtsabschnitte dürfen nur

50 Gr. Brot oder 35 Gr. Mehl *(repeated across card)*

52   GERMANY (?)   Ration card

⟨ **Stadtrat Graz (Ernährungsamt).** ⟩

Giltig bis auf weiteres.   **Milchkarte.**
Unübertragbar.

Herr — Frau ....

wohnhaft .... ist berechtigt,

⬛ Liter Voll- oder Flaschenmilch zu
kaufen in der Milchverkaufsstelle

....

Die Partei hat sich einen Tag vor Bezug der Milch bei der
Milchverkaufsstelle anzumelden. Diese Milchkarte berechtigt zum
Bezuge der Milch nur während der in der Milchverkaufsstelle
angegebenen Ausgabezeit. Änderungen in der Zuweisung werden
nur bei Wohnungswechsel vorgenommen.

STADTRAT GRAZ

53   AUSTRIA 1917 (?)   Milk ration card

THE RATIONS. F.E. 12.

1. The position of the Food supply is such that the UTMOST ECONOMY IN THE USE OF ALL KINDS OF FOOD must be observed by all classes and by all persons.

2. In particular it is necessary that the strictest economy should be practised in the use of the staple foods; *bread, flour and other cereals; meat; butter, margarine and lard; and sugar.*

3. The weekly rations of these staple foods, which are stated in the following table for different classes of adults according to their sex and occupation, should on no account be exceeded.

4. Children should receive their reasonable rations of these foods.

Their individual needs differ so greatly that no definite ration is laid down for them.

ADULT RATIONS PER HEAD PER WEEK.

Class.	Bread.	Other cereals.	Meat.	Butter, Margarine, Lard, Oils and Fats.	Sugar.
	lb. oz.	oz.	lb. oz.	oz.	oz.
MEN.					
1. Men on very heavy industrial work or on agricultural work.	8 0				
2. Men on ordinary industrial or other manual work.	7 0				
3. Men unoccupied or on sedentary work.	4 8				
WOMEN.					
4. Women on heavy industrial work or on agricultural work.	5 0	12	2 0	~~44~~ 10	8
5. Women on ordinary industrial work or in domestic service.	4 0				
6. Women unoccupied or on sedentary work.	3 8				

W. & Co. Ltd.—1.000.000—14-12-17.   [P.T.O.

55   BRITAIN December 1917   Leaflet

IF FOUND, RETURN TO ANY FOOD OFFICE.

30 SEP 1918   **MINISTRY OF FOOD.** 35938

NATIONAL RATION BOOK (B).

INSTRUCTIONS.

Read carefully these instructions and the leaflet which will be sent you with this Book.

1. The person named on the reference leaf as the holder of this ration book must write his name and address in the space below, and must write his name and address, and the serial number (printed upside down on the back cover), in the space provided to the left of each page of coupons.

Food Office of ⟨DUMFRIES COUNTY & BURGHS⟩ Date ....
Issue

Signature of Holder ....

Address ....

2. For convenience of writing at the Food Office the Reference Leaf has been put opposite the back cover, and has purposely been printed upside down. It should be carefully examined. If there is any mistake in the entries on the Reference Leaf, the Food Office should be asked to correct it.

3. The holder must register this book at once by getting his retailers for butcher's meat, bacon, butter and margarine, sugar and tea respectively, to write their names and the addresses of their shops in the proper space on the back of the cover. Persons staying in hotels, boarding houses, hostels, schools, and similar establishments should not register their books until they leave the establishment.

4. The ration book may be used only by or on behalf of the holder, to buy rationed food for him, or members of the same household, or guests sharing common meals. It may not be used to buy rationed food for any other persons.

N. 2 (Nov.)   [*Continued on next page.*

54   SCOTLAND September 1918   Ration book

CARTE POUR LE PAIN
Ne pas plier cette Carte, s. v. p.

Comité d'Alimentation du Nord de la France
C. F.

N° 233

Arrondissement de Cambrai

COMMUNE DE RIEUX

Boulanger _Gardez_

	1er jour	2e jour	3e jour
Nombre de pains à distribuer	1/2	1/2	1

Nom _Dhollande Chabois_

Adresse _Rue du Moulin_

Total des personnes composant le Ménage. **2**

Présenter cette carte les

1. — Le pain est distribué dans les locaux choisis par la Mairie et il est interdit de le vendre partout ailleurs. Chaque ménage a donc à aller prendre dans le local indiqué sur sa carte le pain qui lui est accordé et qu'il ne peut obtenir qu'en présentant cette carte sur laquelle une barre doit constater la livraison faite.

5 CAMBRAI, FRANCE   Bread card

STADT MÜNCHEN	STADT MÜNCHEN	STADT MÜNCHEN. Bestellmarke	STADT MÜNCHEN. Bezugsmarke
R 153	R 157	44	44
R 152	R 156	43	43

57 MUNICH   Ration card

Ausweis (Beglaubigungschein)
Mittwoch 16.—52. Woche (15. April bis 29. Dezember 1917)

Herr
Frau

Nürg. 23

verlogt in seinem (ihrem) Haushalte 4 Personen.

Lauf. Nr 605   35545   Brot-Komm. II

58 MODLING, AUSTRIA 1917   Ration card

Bezirk Nr. 9   35514   Sorgfältig aufbewahren.   **A**

Friedrich Stadt Kiel.

Lebensmittelkartenheft

Name: Wohnung: Nr.

Inhalt:
1. 3 Bezugskarten für Brot Nr. 49—60 .. für die Zeit vom
2. Bezugskarte für Aufstrich ....
3.   „   „ Zucker ....
4.   „   „ Mehl ....
5.   „   „ Mühlenfabrikate usw. ....
6.   „   „ Butter und Speisefett ....
7.   „   „ Kartoffeln ....
8. Warenkarte ....

14. August bis
8. Oktober 1919.

35514

9 KIEL, GERMANY August 1919   Provision card

26199

Alle Donne d'Italia

POSTAL CENSORSHIP.

As announced in the Press, pictorial illustrations and photographs of all kinds, whether on postcards addressed to neutral or enemy countries or enclosed in letters so addressed, and whether the illustration itself does or does not represent an object of interest to the enemy, are stopped and returned by the Censor.

W5006—482 50,000 8/16 HWV(P930)

60 ITALY c1916 War Loan booklet

TO THE WOMEN OF ITALY To subscribe to the National Loan is to win; to win is to keep faith with the dead—Nina Sauro. The war we are now waging is a holy one, both for the country and for humanity. As we give the lives of our sons we may less onerously give our money and our jewels—Costanza Garibaldi

61 LONDON August 1916 Returned correspondence slip

AVIS au Public

Dans le but d'enrayer la spéculation et la vente de ses Laits concentrés à des prix exagérés,

LA SOCIÉTÉ

NESTLÉ

a l'honneur d'informer le public consommateur qu'elle a fixé les prix suivants pour la vente au détail :

Lait concentré sucré : 1ʳ65 la boîte
» » non sucré : 1ʳ60 »

Les frais spéciaux (port, camionnage, taxes d'octroi, etc.) que les détaillants ont quelquefois à leur charge peuvent justifier, dans certains cas, une majoration des prix; toutefois cette majoration ne saurait excéder 0.20 cent. par boîte.

62 PARIS August 1914
Press announcement

NOTICE TO THE PUBLIC With a view to curbing speculation and the sale of milk concentrates at inflated prices, the Nestlé company has the honour to inform the consuming public that it has fixed the following prices for retail sale: Sweetened condensed milk 1.65fr per tin; unsweetened, 1.60fr per tin. Special costs (port handling, transport, etc) which retailers may sometimes incur may in certain cases justify an increase in price. The increase should not, however, exceed 20 centimes per tin.

Not for Publication

Suspicious Vessels Notice No. 3.

FISHERY BOARD FOR SCOTLAND.

Suspicious Vessels in North Sea.

NOTICE TO SKIPPERS OF FISHING VESSELS.

Skippers of fishing vessels are requested to keep a sharp look out for any fishing vessel named in the following Lists :—

A. Vessels sold to Foreign Owners before the outbreak of the War or subsequently.		B. Vessels reported as having been captured or sunk by the Enemy.		C. Vessels reported as missing.	
Strathfillan	A. 63	Wigtoft	R.N. 19	Nelson	G.Y. 41
Helen Macgregor	A. 439	Porpoise	R.N. 23	Ceylon	G.Y. 366
Philip Maxsted	A. 537	Walrus	R.N. 31	Jacana	L.L. 61
Locost	A. 564	Skirbeck	R.N. 81		
Neptune	F.D. 124	Flavian	R.N. 86		
Moth	F.D. 167	Julian	R.N. 88		
Hornet	F.D. 168	Indian	R.N. 90		
Wasp	F.D. 169	Kesteven	R.N. 173		
Velia	F.D. 229	Lindsey	R.N. 174		
Aldgate	G.Y. 776	Seti	G.Y. 72		
Guernsey	H. 271	Lobelia	G.Y. 93		
Alderney	H. 273	Chameleon	G.Y. 105		
Wales	H. 282	Argonaut	G.Y. 189		
Ontario	H. 294	Zenobia	G.Y. 277		
Vancouver	H. 299	Rideo	G.Y. 314		
Ixia	M. 131	Pegasus	G.Y. 443		
		Rhine	G.Y. 518		
		St. Cuthbert	G.Y. 519		
		Capricornus	G.Y. 750		
		Valiant	G.Y. 1178		
		Pollux	G.Y. 1184		
		Harrier	G.Y. 1192		
		Mersey	G.Y. 1196		

[OVER.

It is possible that some of these boats, still bearing their British names and port marks, may be used by the enemy as Mine-layers, or for the purposes of spying.

Any Skipper who in the course of fishing sees any of the above-mentioned vessels or any other vessel known to have been reported as missing or captured, should, if the vessel is still bearing British marks :—

1. Either notify the fact, with full particulars as to the place and time, to any naval vessel which may be in the vicinity, or which he may see on his way to port;

2. Or, he should, in the absence of such vessels, immediately return to the nearest port and inform the Naval Authorities there, or, if he can do so more quickly, the Fishery Officer, who will immediately pass on the report to the Naval Authorities.

It is of the utmost importance that the intelligence should be conveyed without delay, for otherwise it would not be possible for measures to be taken to overhaul the Suspicious Vessel.

Any additions to or deletions from the lists of vessels given above will be notified by means of Supplementary Notices issued for the purpose.

All enemy vessels, whether previously British owned or not, and any craft acting in a suspicious manner should, of course, be promptly reported.

David T. Jones

FISHERY-BOARD FOR SCOTLAND,
EDINBURGH, *16th October* 1914.

Secretary.

63 EDINBURGH October 1914 Leaflet

THE WAR.

NOTICE.

Recipients of Relief from the National Relief Fund, or from any other source, are respectfully informed that they will not be served in this establishment with anything more than necessary refreshment.

Issued by the authority of the Wholesale and Retail Licensed Trade Associations in the Greater Birmingham Area, and to be PROMINENTLY displayed in the windows, and about Licensed Houses.

64 LONDON 1914 Notice

THE SAILORS DAY

65 BRITAIN c1915 Charity ba

TIME FOR
ONE MORE

MITCHELL'S
"GOLDEN DAWN"
CIGARETTES.

6 BRITAIN 1914 Showcard

THIS IS A ✠ PIECE OF
GENUINE
ZEPPELIN WIRE,
FROM THE FIRST ZEPPELIN BROUGHT
DOWN AT CUFFLEY IN ESSEX
SEPT. 3RD., 1916.

Given by H.M. War Office exclusively to the
British Red Cross Society.

67 BRITAIN September 1916
Charity souvenir

STIRRING
TIMES

Fry's PURE
BREAKFAST
COCOA

"In Itself a Perfect Food"

68 BRITAIN c1914 Press advertisement

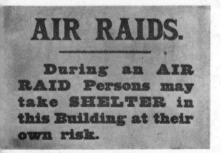

AIR RAIDS.

**During an AIR
RAID Persons may
take SHELTER in
this Building at their
own risk.**

9 LONDON 1915 Notice

NOTICE

Arrangements have been made that warning of a threatened air raid will be communicated by the Military Authorities to this theatre.

On receipt of any such warning the audience will be informed, with a view to enable persons who may wish to proceed home, to do so.

The warning will be communicated, so far as possible, at least 20 minutes before any actual attack can take place. There will, therefore, be no cause for alarm or undue haste.

Those who decide to leave are warned not to loiter about the streets, and if bombardment or gunfire commences before they reach home, they should at once take cover.

By Order of The Commissioner of Police of the Metropolis. *New Scotland Yard, S.W.*

70 LONDON 1915 Theatre programme notice

72 RUSSIA c1915 Poster

Subscribe to the 5¼% War Loan
and pave the way to Victory!

71 PARIS December 1915 Poster

SOLDIER'S DAY December 25 and 26 1915 Organized by Parliament

76 BRITAIN 1914 Poster

TO THE
YOUNG WOMEN
OF LONDON

Is your "Best Boy" wearing Khaki? If not don't YOU THINK he should be?

If he does not think that you and your country are worth fighting for—do you think he is WORTHY of you?

Don't pity the girl who is alone—her young man is probably a soldier—fighting for her and her country—and for YOU.

If your young man neglects his duty to his King and Country, the time may come when he will NEGLECT YOU.

Think it over—then ask him to

JOIN THE ARMY TO-DAY

LONDON 1915   Poster

74   ITALY c1917   Poster

NATIONAL LOAN For the Country, my eyes; for Peace, your money

75   AUSTRIA c1917   Poster

Subscribe to the Sixth War Loan

"Have you room in your heart for us."

Motherless Children of France, Inc.

UNITED STATES (?)   Poster

Have you room in your heart for us?

78   BRITAIN c1915   Poster

79   UNITED STATES c1917   Poster

For our independence, down with murderers; up with democracy! Czechoslovak Army

Are you ready for the next zeppelin raid? At any moment the zeppelins may come. Your house may be reached by their bombs. The airships carry asphyxiating missiles. Put yourself and yours out of danger by getting the 'Civilian' respirator mask (patented). This mask offers absolute protection against the poisonous gases emitted by the German aviators. Made in a pliable fabric to mould itself exactly to the head . . . and the filter pad has been approved by the English Academy of medicine. . . .

Etes-vous prêts pour le prochain raid des Zeppelins?

A tout moment les Zeppelins peuvent venir. Votre maison peut être atteinte par leurs bombes. Les dirigeables allemands transportent des engins asphyxiants. Mettez-vous ainsi que les vôtres à l'abri de leurs dangers en vous procurant

LE MASQUE RESPIRATEUR
Le "CIVILIAN"
(Breveté)

Ce masque est d'une protection absolue contre les gaz empoisonnés émis par les bombes des aviateurs allemands. Fait en tissu souple pour se mouler exactement sur la tête, il s'adapte sans attaches, agrafes ou autres, est muni pour la vue d'un dispositif transparent et incombustible, et le tampon filtreur de gaz a été approuvé par l'Académie de Médecine anglaise. Il est vendu dans une enveloppe imperméable et se porte, roulé, dans la poche ou dans un sac à main.

Prix : 4 fr. 50, franco

Insister pour avoir le "CIVILIAN" et n'en acceptez pas d'autres. En vente *aux Galeries Lafayette.* Si votre fournisseur ordinaire ne le tenait pas encore, il vous suffira pour en obtenir un franco d'envoyer la somme de 4 fr. 75 à

MM. D. HARPER Cᵒ Lᵗᵈ, 258-262, Holloway Road, Londres, N.

80   PARIS 1915   Press advertisement

81   BRITAIN c1917   Showcard

SEMPRE AVANTI !!

82   ITALY c1915   Patriotic print

Always onwards

COUNTY OF CAMBRIDGE.
DEFENCE OF THE REALM.
Important Notice.

SHOOTING HOMING PIGEONS.

I have been directed to make known that the use of Homing Pigeons by the Admiralty has been made known by publication in the Press of the following Notice :—

"It has been decided to use Carrier Pigeons for certain purposes in connection with His Majesty's Service. The Public are therefore requested to refrain from shooting or otherwise interfering with Carrier Pigeons."

It occasionally happens, when bearing a message, birds may drop and be captured or killed. As there will be an ownership in pigeons used on His Majesty's Service, whoever appropriates them will be liable to a heavy penalty. If by chance any such exhausted or untrained "homer" carrying a message should be captured or come into possession of any person this should be notified to the Police, who will at once telegraph to the Admiralty copy of the message and the ring number, and by first post afterwards transmit the message itself to the Admiralty, London, and detain the bird until owned.

The pigeons to be used in this service will occasionally be sent to distant railway stations and liberated for exercising purposes.

CHARLES STRETTEN, M.V.O.,

County Constabulary Office, Cambridge. 30th November, 1914. Chief Constable of Cambridgeshire.

EXPRESS PRINTING WORKS, KING STREET, CAMBRIDGE.

83   CAMBRIDGE, November 1914   Notic

86   GERMAN
Show

Breakth
'Ahead for the E

Worth Knowing

On the opposite page we show two sizes of high explosive shells which can be produced from the bar on our 4½" PEDESTAL BASE MACHINE (see cut on opposite page).

On this machine we can finish a 13-lb. shell all over as it appears from very tough material from which shells are made, in 24 minutes, and from ordinary machine steel in 17 minutes.

The 18-lb. shell in 30 minutes, or from regular machine steel in 22 minutes.

When you figure about $1.00 per day for operating this machine, you can then arrive at the actual labor cost for producing the piece.

We are going to say a little more—something which might be interesting. The following is a description of the 13- and 18-lb. high explosive shells which are now being used so extensively in the war to replace common shrapnel.

The material is high in tensile strength and VERY SPECIAL and has a tendency to fracture into small pieces upon the explosion of the shell. The timing of the fuse for this shell is similar to the shrapnel shell, but it differs in that two explosive acids are used to explode the shell in the large cavity. The combination of these two acids causes terrific explosion, having more power than anything of its kind yet used. Fragments become coated with these acids in exploding and wounds caused by them mean death in terrible agony within four hours if not attended to immediately.

From what we are able to learn of conditions in the trenches, it is not possible to get medical assistance to anyone in time to prevent fatal results. It is necessary to immediately cauterize the wound if in the body or head, or to amputate if in the limbs, as there seems to be no antidote that will counteract the poison.

It can be seen from this that this shell is more effective than the regular shrapnel, since the wounds caused by shrapnel balls and fragments in the muscles are not as dangerous as they have no poisonous element making prompt attention necessary.

CLEVELAND AUTOMATIC MACHINE COMPANY
Cleveland, Ohio, U. S. A.

UNITED STATES May 1915   Press advertisement

Heizbarer ⊞ Steigbügel
D.R.P.

"Reiterfreude"

Eine Wohltat für jeden Reiter-soldaten im Felde
Preis pro Paar
inkl. Kohle ....M. **11.50**
Erhältlich überall. . Wo nicht, wende man sich an den alleinigen Fabrikanten
C. MAQUET G. m. b. H., **HEIDELBERG**

Heatable stirrups. A boon to every cavalryman in the field. Price per pair, including charcoal, 11.50 marks. Obtainable everywhere. Where not, apply to sole manufacturers . . .

85   GERMANY 1914   Press advertisement

Dr Gentner's Seifenpulver Schneekönig

Gewidmet von Carl Gentner Göppingen.

Durchbruch „Ran an den Feind"

P.T.

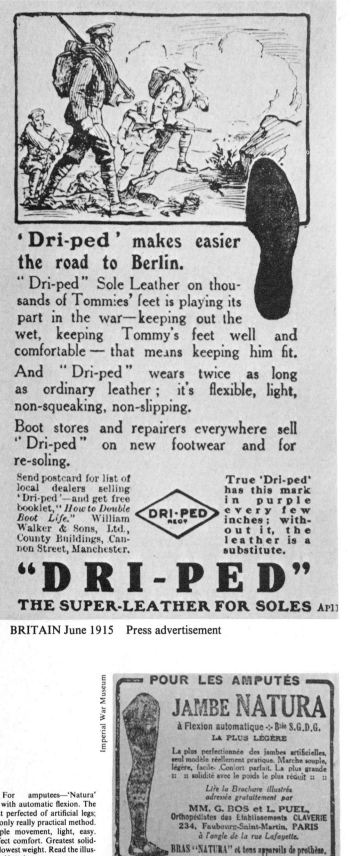

'Dri-ped' makes easier the road to Berlin.

"Dri-ped" Sole Leather on thousands of Tommies' feet is playing its part in the war—keeping out the wet, keeping Tommy's feet well and comfortable — that means keeping him fit.

And "Dri-ped" wears twice as long as ordinary leather; it's flexible, light, non-squeaking, non-slipping.

Boot stores and repairers everywhere sell "Dri-ped" on new footwear and for re-soling.

Send postcard for list of local dealers selling 'Dri-ped'—and get free booklet, "How to Double Boot Life." William Walker & Sons, Ltd., County Buildings, Cannon Street, Manchester.

DRI·PED REGD

True 'Dri-ped' has this mark in purple every few inches; without it, the leather is a substitute.

"DRI-PED"
THE SUPER-LEATHER FOR SOLES Ap11

87 BRITAIN June 1915 Press advertisement

For amputees—'Natura' leg, with automatic flexion. The most perfected of artificial legs; the only really practical method. Supple movement, light, easy. Perfect comfort. Greatest solidity, lowest weight. Read the illustrated brochure. . . .

POUR LES AMPUTÉS

JAMBE NATURA
à Flexion automatique -:- B^{te} S.G.D.G.
LA PLUS LÉGÈRE

La plus perfectionnée des jambes artificielles, seul modèle réellement pratique. Marche souple, légère, facile. Confort parfait. La plus grande :: solidité avec le poids le plus réduit ::

Lise la Brochure illustrée
adressée gratuitement par
MM. G. BOS et L. PUEL,
Orthopédistes des Etablissements CLAVERIE
234, Faubourg-Saint-Martin, PARIS
à l'angle de la rue Lafayette.

BRAS "NATURA" et tous appareils de prothèse.

88 PARIS 1914 Press advertisement

'FROG'S GREASE' Army-approved oil leather grease; keeps the leather soft and waterproof, the feet warm and dr

„Frosch‑Fett
Vorschriftsmäss. Armee-Tranlederfett
hält das Leder weich &
wasserdicht, die Füsse
warm und trocken!
Original Doseo

Marke "Froschkönig"
Tran-Lederfett
Schafft weiches wasserdichtes Leder

Werner & Mertz   Mainz & Wien

Hier in Feldpost-   Packó haben

89 GERMANY/AUSTRIA 1915 Poster

90   BRITAIN 1915   Press advertisement

Imperial War Museum

SANATOGEN provides a power reserve on which overtaxed nerve and body resources may draw. For our soldiers it offers an unequalled potential for the maintaining of health and powers of resistance . . . Available in special Field Service Pack at all chemists. . . . [This product, though it continued in Britain during the war in an anglicized version, originated in Germany.]

Sanatogen

Von 21000 Ärzten anerkanntes Kräftigungsmittel für Körper und Nerven. Sanatogen schafft einen Kräftevorrat, aus dem jeder Mehrverbrauch an Körper- und Nervenkraft ersetzt werden kann. So bietet es also auch für unsere Krieger eine unvergleichliche Möglichkeit zur Erhaltung der Gesundheit und Widerstandskraft. — Sanatogen-Feldpostbrief-Packungen in allen Apotheken und Drogerien. — Die Sanatogen-Werke, Berlin SW. 48 B/9, Friedrichstrasse 231, versenden kostenlos aufklärende Schriften über:

Sanatogen als Kräftigungsmittel

1. bei Nervenleiden	3. bei Magen- und Darmleiden	6. bei Kinderkrankheiten
2. **bei Rekonvaleszenz** und Schwächezuständen aller Art	4. bei Lungenleiden	7. bei Frauenleiden
	5. bei Bleichsucht und Blutarmut	8. bei Ernähruungsstörungen
	ferner 9. Merkblatt für werdende Mütter und Wöchnerinnen.	

Wer Sanatogen noch nicht kennt, **verlange eine Gratisprobe** von der obengenannten Firma.

91   GERMANY 1914   Press advertisement

JEU DES QUATRARMES BREVETÉ S.G.D.G.

PLUS AMUSANT QUE LES DAMES   PLUS SIMPLE QUE LES ÉCHECS

The game of 'FOURARMS' —more amusing than draughts, simpler than chess

92   FRANCE c1915   Boxed game label

93 FRANCE 1914 Children's cutout

94 BRITAIN 1914-15 Cigarette cards

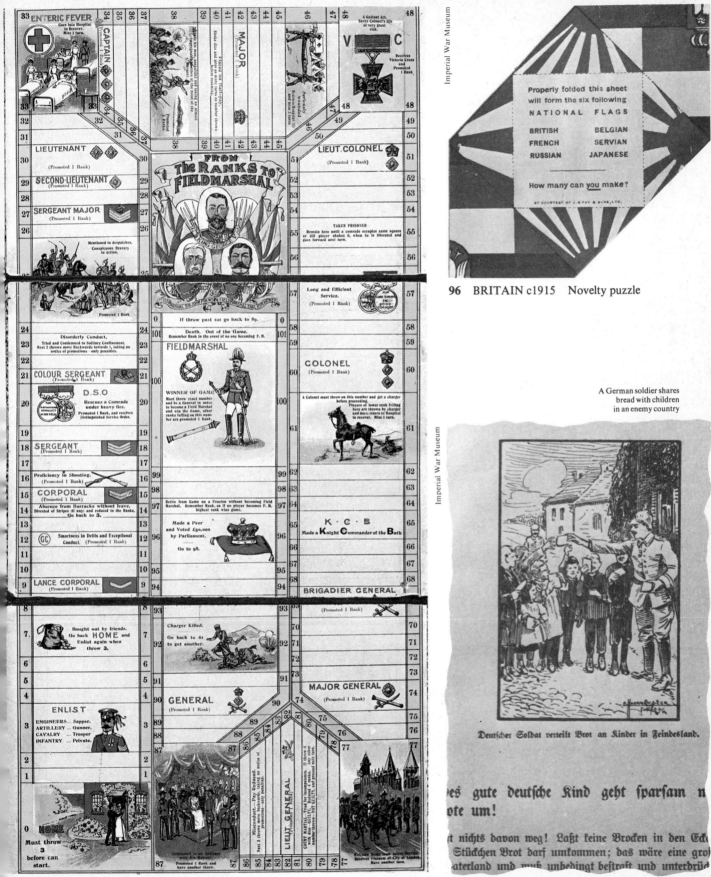

96 BRITAIN c1915   Novelty puzzle

Properly folded this sheet will form the six following NATIONAL FLAGS

BRITISH   BELGIAN
FRENCH   SERVIAN
RUSSIAN   JAPANESE

How many can you make?

BY COURTESY OF J. S. FRY & SONS, LTD.

A German soldier shares bread with children in an enemy country

Deutscher Soldat verteilt Brot an Kinder in Feindesland.

95 BRITAIN 1914   Board game

97 GERMANY c1915   Children's book illustration

Frühling im Winter.

98 BERLIN c1915 Patriotic print
Spring in Winter

SAVE HIS LIFE!

THE
DAYFIELD BODY SHIELD

is proof against bayonet, sword, and lance. It is also proof against spent bullets, shrapnel, shell-splinters and grenades. The "Dayfield" is a *tested* and *proved* life-protector, absolutely fulfilling every claim made for it.

> **SIR HIRAM MAXIM says:—**
> *Fully twenty-five per cent. of the casualties we have met so far would have been prevented by the use of this shield.*

The "Dayfield" Shield is worn under the tunic. It is light in weight (29 oz.), comfortable in wear, and in no way impedes action. Four specially toughened metal plates, strengthened at the joinings by steel strips, explain the "Dayfield" resistive power. The shield is covered with Khaki drill.

SEND 'HIM' A DAYFIELD NOW!

Carriage Paid in British Isles	..	..	**21/6**
Carriage paid to the Front ..	..	..	**22/6**

DOUBLE SHIELD to protect front & back.

Carriage Paid in British Isles	..	..	**53/6**
Carriage Paid to the Front ..	..	..	**55/-**

Of Military Outfitters & Stores or direct

THE WHITFIELD MANUFACTURING CO., LTD.,

Vernon House, Sicilian Avenue, Southampton Row, London, W.C.,

where Models and Testimonials can be seen.

Victory!

British Airmen are winning the supremacy of the air, as their fore-fathers won the supremacy of the sea. Indomitable pluck, the true sporting spirit, and nerves of steel are as indispensable to victory as ever.

The nation with the best nerves will win. Good nerves are the outcome of continuous good health and regular daily habits. The system must be as regularly cleansed as the body. It is the daily habit of Kruschen Salts that keeps you always fit and well—that cleanses the body of impurities and gives you a sense of alertness and vigour.

The habit is an easy one to acquire, and the consequences of that habit are to be found in renewed vigour, a cheerful outlook on life, and all the blessings of constant health.

Kruschen Salts, taken daily, are as refreshing and invigorating to the nervous system as a morning plunge into fresh sea water. They *revitalize* you and clear away the dull, jaded feeling that is a sure augury of liver troubles.

Kruschen Salts
MAKERS ESTABLISHED IN MANCHESTER 1754.
ENTIRELY BRITISH FOR 160 YEARS

Sole Manufacturers : E. GRIFFITHS HUGHES (KRUSCHEN), Ltd., 68, Deansgate Arcade, MANCHESTER.

Sold by all Chemists at 1/6 per Bottle.

The ingredients of Kruschen Salts are necessary for healthy life. Your body must, of necessity, obtain these ingredients from somewhere, or you could not live. Normally your system should extract these vital salts from your food—meat, bread, fruit, vegetables, milk, eggs, and so on; but as a matter of fact, owing to impaired digestion, errors of diet, overwork, anxiety, worry, sedentary occupation, and many other causes, your system does not extract from food the correct proportions of these essential life-giving salts. And what follows? Depression, or headaches or constipation, or disordered liver, or inactive kidneys, or Rheumatism, or Gout or Sciatica, or Lumbago, or Eczema—many of which arise from excess of Uric Acid, which is the cause of more trouble than many people suspect.

Kruschen Salts should be your safeguard. Besides cleansing the body of impurities gently, surely, and painlessly, they possess a wonderful power of giving new life and vitality to the countless millions of cells of which every body is composed. Flesh, blood, cartilage, bone, brain, and nerve are all made up of cells, and every cell requires one or more of the numerous constituents of Kruschen Salts for its healthy life.

warning !

The latest "substitution" trick.

As the market is flooded with inferior imitations of Kruschen Salts we think the public ought to know that **in some shops salesmen are offered a special commission of 3d. a bottle to push a substitute** when Kruschen is asked for. Therefore, when you are offered a substitute, have the courage to insist on Kruschen. A salesman who tries to sell you a substitute is obviously thinking more about his extra commission than your health. If the trick should be tried on you, shun that shop in future and go to an honest chemist.

Mitchell's "*BINNACLE*" Cigarettes.

101   BRITAIN c1914   Showcard

Deutsch sein, heißt stark sein

102   GERMANY c1917
Charity stamp
To be German is to be strong

CLEANSING LONDON.

have heard it from end to end of the Army that "the Londoner has the heart of a lion."

Wave after wave poured forward over the German trench with unconquerable steadiness; they fell, they were wounded, but they waved on their comrades, and it is not only the mothers who bore them but the people of the country that has produced them who are proud of the Island Brood, who have shown truly the metal of their forefathers who won Waterloo and Trafalgar.

Be sure, then, that I am not come out to-day to blacken the character of the British race. I glory in being a son of Britain to-day, and after a week-end with the London Regiments in their different camps I can tell the German Emperor there are plenty more units for him, only too anxious to get at him, on this side of the water.

No! What I have come out to denounce to-day are the villains more mischievous than German spies, who ought to share their fate,

24

CLEANSING LONDON.

who lie in wait to stain the chivalry of our boys, poison their minds, and undermine their characters.

1. For instance, what are we to say to the male hawks who walk up and down this very Piccadilly night by night with twenty or thirty helpless and trembling girls under their surveillance, and who take from them the very money the girls earn by their shame. I am not a bloodthirsty man, but I say shooting is too good for them. I brought in a Bill before the war, and shall bring it in again after the war, which not only raised the age of consent from sixteen to eighteen, but would have made the life of a *souteneur* or bully too much of a hell for him to stay in London.

2. Then side by side with the male hawk as a traitor to his country should be dealt with the writer of lecherous and slimy productions ranking as stage plays. He has the insolence to try and make money out of the weaknesses of our boys. God knows in

25

103   LONDON c1915   *Cleansing London* by the Bishop of London

Die Deutsche Sektmarke unserer großen Zeit

Feist-Feldgrau

Sektkellerei Frankfurt a. M. A.G.

104 GERMANY c1915   Poster

The German Champagne for our Time of Greatness: Feist 'Field-grey'

Army Medical Examiner: "At last a perfect soldier!"

106
UNITED STATES 1916
Cartoon (*The Masses*)

The Appeal of a Poster

BY N. A. JENNINGS

"Huns Kill Women and Children!"
  It was staring him in the face,
Telling the tale in headlines
  Of the deeds of a hellborn race;
Telling of dastards' doings,
  Black murder hurled down from the skies
On nursing babes and mothers—
  Such a slaughter as Germans prize.

"Huns Kill Women and Children!"
  And the words seared into his soul;
His heart grew sick with horror
  At thought of the pitiful toll.
Then rage filled all his being
  And he took an oath then and there,
"Those black fiends must be punished,
  And, by God! I will do my share!"

"Huns Kill Women and Children!"
  With each moment his anger grew;
Grim, determined, jaw hard set,
  He was fighting mad through and through.
Gentle with child or woman,
  Full of courage and fine and clean,
Showing in all his make-up,
  True type of the fighting Marine!

"Huns Kill Women and Children!"
  They are doing it now, to-day!
Murdering Red Cross nurses,
  Dropping bombs on children at play.
Get in the fight to stop them;
  In France men are showing you how;
Join the Marines! Go to it!
  And the time to enlist is NOW!

New York Herald

107   UNITED STATES 1914 (?)
Press poem

4th LIBERTY LOAN

food—don't waste it
1 – use less wheat and meat
2 – buy local foods
3 – serve just enough
4 use what is left

Red Cross War Fund

You'll be uncomfortable without your Honor Button

FOURTH LIBERTY LOAN

during the 4th LIBERTY LOAN

105   UNITED STATES 1918   Poster card

Imperial War Museum

Victoria and Albert Museum

keep these off the U.S.A
Buy more LIBERTY BONDS

108 UNITED STATES 1918 Poster

ONLY THE NAVY CAN STOP THIS

109 UNITED STATES 1917 Poster

Victoria and Albert Museum

BUY UNITED STATES GOVERNMENT WAR SAVINGS STAMPS

W·S·S For Sale Here

Your money back with interest from the UNITED STATES TREASURY

110 UNITED STATES c1917 Poster

Victoria and Albert Museum

U.S. NAVY

"Here he is, Sir."
We need him and you too!
Navy Recruiting Station

111 UNITED STATES 1917 Poster

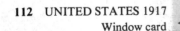

I OWN A LIBERTY BOND

Wear a United States Government
Bond Holder's Button
IT IS A BADGE OF HONOR

112 UNITED STATES 1917
Window card

Victoria and Albert Museum

SEND OFF DAY
TO THE NEW YORK NATIONAL GUARD

113 UNITED STATES 1917 Poster

"Those of you who have loved ones in France must write write, write". • • •
Gen'l Pershing

HART SCHAFFNER & MARX
Good Clothes Makers

NOTHING is to be written on this side except the date and signature of the sender. Sentences not required may be erased. If anything else is added the post card will be destroyed.

I am quite well.

I have been admitted into hospital

{ sick } and am going on well.
{ wounded } and hope to be discharged soon.

I am being sent down to the base.

I have received your { letter dated_____
{ telegram ,, _____
{ parcel ,, _____

Letter follows at first opportunity.

I have received no letter from you
{ lately.
{ for a long time.

Signature }
only. }

Date_____

[Postage must be prepaid on any letter or post card addressed to the sender of this card.]

(25540) Wt.W3497-293 1,130m. 6/15 M.R.Co.,Ltd.

115 BRITAIN June 1916 Field Service card

116 BRITAIN c1915 Postcard

117 AUSTRIA (?) Postcard

In the firing line

118   FRANCE c1915   Postcard   The Ambulance Dog

LE CHIEN AMBULANCIER

119   GERMANY c1915   Postcard
Greetings

Auf dieser Karte darf sonst nichts mitgeteilt werden.

Ezen a levelezőlapon mást nem szabad közölni.

Na tomto lístku nesmí se nic jiného sděliti.

Pe această carte nu este dartat a se face alte împărtăşiri.

Ich bin gesund und es geht mir gut.
Egészséges vagyok és jól érzem magamat.
Jsem zdráv a daří se mně dobře.
Jestem zdrów i powodzi mi się dobrze.
Я с здоров і менї веде ся добре.
Sono sano e sto bene.
Jaz sem zdrav in se mi dobro godi.
Zdrav sam i dobro mi je.
Sunt sănătos şi îmi merge bine.

Na ovoj dopisnici ne smije se inače ništa saopćiti.

Na téj kartce nie wolno nic więcej dopisać.

Na tej dopisnici se ne sme ničesar drugega prijavljati.

Su questa cartolina non si dovrà fare ulteriori comunicazioni.

На сїй картцї не вїлно нїчо бїльш повідомляти.

120   CENTRAL POWERS (?)   Multilingual field service card

I am well, and all goes
well with me
Nothing further may be
communicated on this card

121   GERMANY 1914   Postcard   I had a Comrade . . .

PRESENT LOCATION
UNCERTAIN.

LONDON.W.C.
5. 15 PM
OCT 3 16B

Wounded

B.E.F.

122   BRITAIN 1916   Postal cover

or petroleum and ignited. It has been found in practice that 15 gallons of paraffin are required for a pyre containing 12 corpses; cremation should be complete in from 10 to 12 hours.

C. *Treatment of Bodies Exposed in the Open which cannot be Buried or Cremated.*—Bodies in a state of putrefaction lying out in advance of the trenches which cannot be buried or cremated owing to hostile fire, or bodies uncovered in parapets of trenches where they have been hastily buried often give rise to considerable nuisance. They should be dealt with in the following manner:—

(i) *Bodies in the Open.*—Deodorants will be found useful. The bodies may be sprayed with solution C, and if sufficient time is available the clothes should be ripped up so that the solution may be applied to the whole body, particularly in the region of the abdomen, or the bodies can be covered with quick-lime, powdered sulphate of iron, or a mixture of 80 lbs. lime freshly slaked, 11 lbs. sulphate of iron and $\frac{1}{2}$ lb. salt.

Spraying with 5 per cent. cresol or with petrol is also useful in allaying putrefaction and preventing smell.

Corpses in front of the trenches out of reach can be sprayed by means of No. 7 spray or can be drawn in by means of a grappling iron.

(ii) *Bodies in Walls of Trenches, &c.*—Dead bodies and remains of animals in the sides and walls of trenches, mine craters, &c., where removal is impossible should be treated with chloride of lime, quick-lime or sprayed with cresol or solution C and then isolated either by means of boarding filled in with earth and chloride of lime or by sandbags soaked in heavy petroleum oil.

D. *Disposal of Animals.*—Large animals such as horses are difficult to bury or cremate. They should first be eviscerated and the viscera buried. The carcase should then be buried or burnt. This will be facilitated if the carcase is first cut into convenient pieces. If this is not feasible, the carcase should be covered with earth, or if this is not practicable paraffin should be poured over it and ignited.

108. BURIAL OF CARCASES IN MANURE.

An ample supply of manure is essential for the success of this process. Where such is available the burial of carcases in manure is a satisfactory method of disposal.

123   BRITAIN c1917   Page from Military Hygiene instruction manual

127   GERMANY 1914   Panoramic p[...]

their Bangalore Torpedoes which blew the German barbed wire to bits.

One minute later at 12.21 they had entered the German Trench.

The Huns put up a great fight, our men flung bombs into the trench before they jumped in, but three or four Huns hopped over their own parapet and commenced bombing our men in their trench.

A lot of our Riflemen were specially armed with revolvers and they soon disposed of these.

Our men were armed with knobkerries also and they smashed a few German skulls in.

Murray an officer in our Company, caught a great big Hun about a foot taller than himself a knock-out blow with his fists, and then trampled his face in with his feet.

124   BRITAIN 1916   War diary

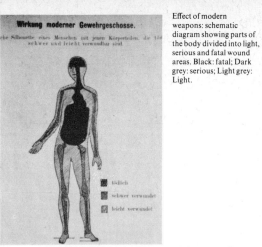

Effect of modern weapons: schematic diagram showing parts of the body divided into light, serious and fatal wound areas. Black: fatal; Dark grey: serious; Light grey: Light.

taught to point at two or more parts of the body, e. g., "First at the nose, then at the right thigh—point."

To practise action against a retreating foe, turn the inside ranks about and let them "rest." Show the position of the kidneys (small of the back, either side of the spine) and make the outside ranks point at those of the inside ranks, and *vice versa.*

23. Vulnerable parts of the body. If possible, the point of the bayonet should be directed against an opponent's throat, especially in *corps à corps* fighting, as the point will enter easily and make a fatal wound on penetrating a few inches and, being near the eyes, makes an opponent "funk." Other vulnerable and usually exposed parts are the face, chest, lower abdomen and thighs, and the region of the kidneys when the back is turned. Four to six inches' penetration is sufficient to incapacitate and allow for a quick withdrawal, whereas if a bayonet is driven home too far it is often impossible to with-

[169]

125   GERMANY c1917   Wound diagram   **126   UNITED STATES 1918   Extract from Military Training Manual**

Conquest of Antwerp, October 9 1914

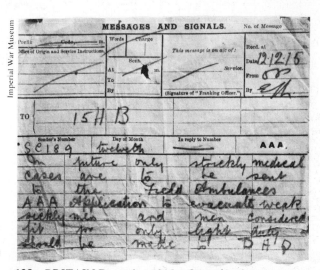

128   BRITAIN December 1915   Operational message

N.B.—This Form must accompany any inquiry respecting this Telegram.

POST OFFICE TELEGRAPHS.

Office Stamp.

If the Receiver of an Inland Telegram doubts its accuracy, he may have it repeated on payment of half the amount originally paid for its transmission, any fraction of 1d. less than ½d. being reckoned as ½d.; and if it be found that there was any inaccuracy, the amount paid for repetition will be refunded. Special conditions are applicable to the repetition of Foreign Telegrams.

Office of Origin and Service Instructions.

TEIGNMOUTH 30 AP 16

Charges to pay

OHMS

War Office London   Handed in at 8 o-   M.   Received here at 8 44 2 M.

TO   Cooke Grandors Teignmouth Devon

Deeply regret to inform you that Capt E R Cooke Irish Fusiliers was killed in action 26th april Lord Kitchener Expresses his Sympathy Secretary War Office

129   BRITAIN April 1916   Telegram

Für die vielen, wohltuenden Beweise der Teilnahme, die wir bei dem Heldentod unseres lieben, hoffnungsvollen Sohnes, Bruders, Enkels und Neffen

Friedrich

in so reichem Maße erfahren durften, sagen wir auf diesem Wege innigen Dank.

Kaiserslautern, den 7. Juli 1917.

Familie Adolf Beisecker.

130   KAISERSLAUTERN, GERMANY July 1917
Condolence acknowledgement card

For the many comforting expressions of sympathy, received in such rich abundance at the heroic death of our beloved son, brother, grand-child and nephew, Friedrich, we convey sincerest thanks. . . .

Auf dem Schlachtfelde bei Ypern erlitt am 29. Dezember, im Alter von kaum 18 Jahren, unser lieber Sohn und Bruder

Sigwart Wertheimer

Kriegsfreiwilliger im Res.-Feld-Art.-Regt. No. 54
Inhaber des Eisernen Kreuzes
und der Silbernen Tapferkeits-Medaille

den Tod fürs Vaterland.

Ludwigsburg, 31. Dezember 1915.

In tiefem Schmerz:

Die Eltern: **Simon Wertheimer**
Selma Wertheimer, geb. Weis
Der Bruder **Ernst Wertheimer.**

E1587

On the battlefield of Ypres on December 29 1915, at barely 18 years of age, our beloved son and brother Sigwart Wertheimer laid down his life for the Fatherland. In deepest grief: his parents . . . his brother. . . .

131   LUDWIGSBURG, GERMANY December 1915
Death notice

132 BRITAIN 1917
Mourning Christmas card

133 BRITAIN June 1916
Condolence acknowledgement card

(Sad memories crowding thick and fast
Bring scenes, how different, of the past.
O Thou, our help and hope and guide,
Bless all who mourn this Christmastide)

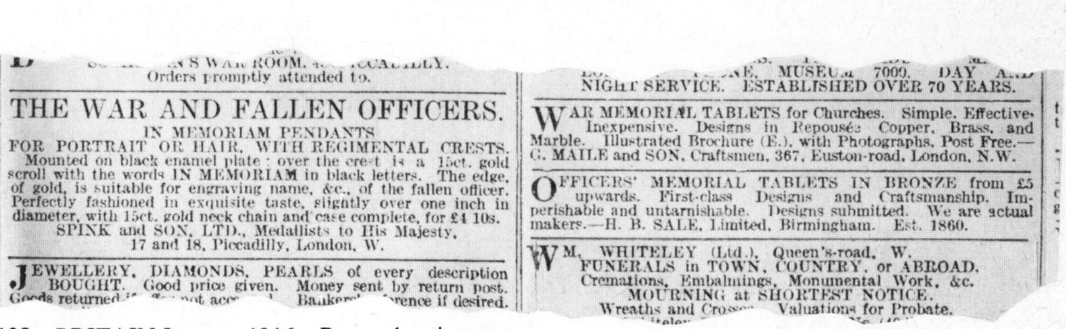

Mrs Parker

returns sincere thanks to

Mr Graham

for his kind expressions of sympathy,

which she deeply appreciates,

in her irreparable loss.

4, Greycoat Gardens.
Westminster. S.W.   *June. 1916.*

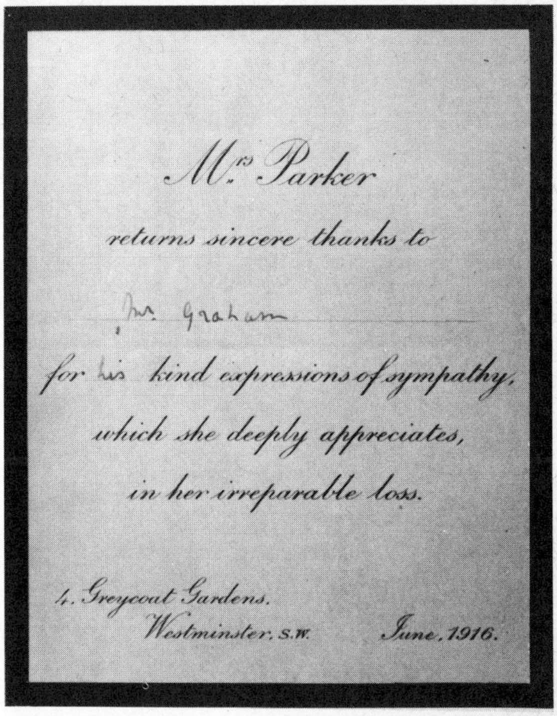

134 GERMANY 1916 Poster

War Memorial Exhibition,
Town Hall, Leipzig

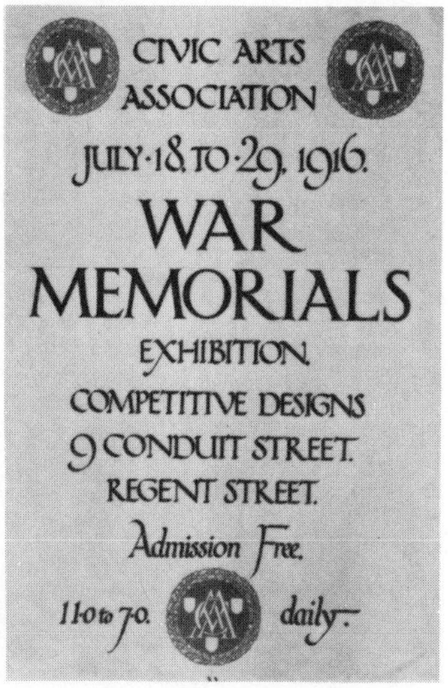

135 BRITAIN 1916 Poster

136 AUSTRIA 1917 Poster

Subscribe to the Sixth War Loan

137 BRITAIN 1915 Poster

138 BRITAIN January 1916 Press advertisements

BUCKINGHAM PALACE.

I join with my grateful people
in sending you this memorial
of a brave life given for others
in the Great War.

George R.I.

139 BRITAIN 1919

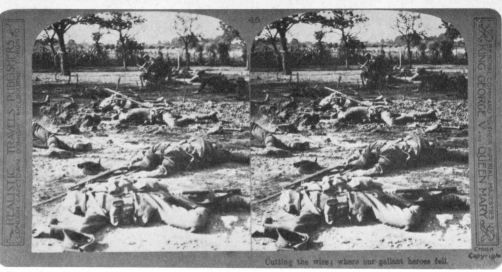

Cutting the wire; where our gallant heroes fell.

140 BRITAIN c1915 Stereoscopic view-card

'And we ought to lay down our lives for the brethren' 1 John, 3,15. In memory of [. . . . .].
He died for the Fatherland on [. . . . .]. [Signed] William R (Memorial card for
dependants of our fallen heroes)

141 GERMANY c1918 Memorial print

Wir sollen auch unser Leben
für die Brüder lassen
1.Joh. 3,15.

Zum Gedächtnis des

Er starb fürs Vaterland
am

Gedenkblatt für die Angehörigen unserer gefallenen Helden.
Ausgeführt im Auftrage des Kaisers von Prof. Emil Doepler d. J.

143 GERMANY c1915 Memorial print

HERBERT CHARLES
COTSWORTH

142 BRITAIN 1919 Memorial plaque

PATRIA

AUX MÈRES AUX VEUVES
DES HÉROS MORTS PIEUSEMENT
POUR LA PATRIE

144 FRANCE 1915 **Memorial print** To the mothers and widows of heroes who laid down their lives for their country

145 BRITAIN May 1916 *Punch* cartoon

146 ITALY June 1917 Magazine cover

I beg leave to report,
your majesty, that
the zeppelins have now gone

147 GERMANY 1916 *Simplicissimus* cartoon

·W·P·

148 GERMANY 1916 Magazine cover

149 BRITAIN c1916 Frostbite ointment

News-lies of our enemy: 'An absolutely reliable source reports "The Germans in Belgium are completely surrounded"' — Daily Telegraph, London; 'The stupid Germans advanced in closed ranks against a solid phalanx of camouflaged French cannon—and were of course completely wiped out.'—Illustrated London News

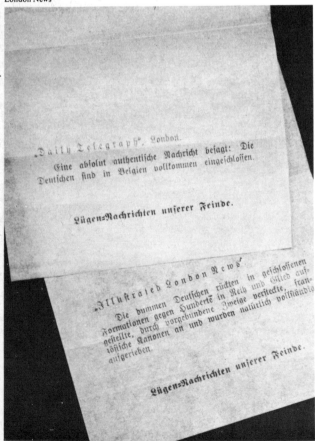

150 GERMANY c1914 'Enemy propaganda' lavatory paper

151 BRITAIN 1915 'Ole Bill' cartoon

Look here, old girl, we've been at war with each other for nigh on twenty years—and all this fuss about *two years!*

152 GERMANY August 1916 *Simplicissimus* joke

„Aeuer, Korl, fett di doch man lewer up dat nige Sofa!"

153   GERMANY 1915   Album cartoon   Come on, Charlie, come and sit on our new sofa

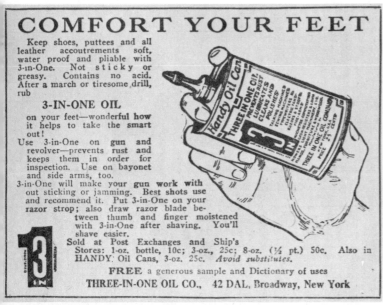

COMFORT YOUR FEET

Keep shoes, puttees and all leather accoutrements soft, water proof and pliable with 3-in-One. Not sticky or greasy. Contains no acid. After a march or tiresome drill, rub

3-IN-ONE OIL

on your feet—wonderful how it helps to take the smart out!

Use 3-in-One on gun and revolver—prevents rust and keeps them in order for inspection. Use on bayonet and side arms, too.

3-in-One will make your gun work without sticking or jamming. Best shots use and recommend it. Put 3-in-One on your razor strop; also draw razor blade between thumb and finger moistened with 3-in-One after shaving. You'll shave easier.

Sold at Post Exchanges and Ship's Stores: 1-oz. bottle, 10c; 3-oz., 25c; 8-oz. (½ pt.) 50c. Also in HANDY Oil Cans, 3-oz. 25c. *Avoid substitutes.*

FREE a generous sample and Dictionary of uses

THREE-IN-ONE OIL CO., 42 DAL, Broadway, New York

154   UNITED STATES 1917   Press advertisement

From London Opinion

Nurse (to badly wounded soldiers who have complained of their food): "You men don't seem to know there's a war on."

155   BRITAIN April 1918   *London Opinion* joke

THE WELL-WISHER'S GIFT 'Silk socks . . . I must
write and thank her!'
'Certainly must. You'll never get a sore throat with that lot
round your neck.'

156   GERMANY c1915   Children's book illustration

Ch. Genty

157   FRANCE March 1917   *La Baïonnette* joke

158   BRITAIN c1915   Press advertisement

159   FRANCE   Magazine 1917

Struck by a bullet, Innerkofler fell back into the abyss

HOW WE BEAT BACK THE HUNS.

BELGIUM TRENCH MORTAR.
Used in the trenches for firing what are known as "Plum Puddings," spherical projectiles with time fuses.
FIND. KING ALBERT.

HOW WE BEAT BACK THE HUNS

BRITISH 6" HOWITZER.
Short, wide-mouthed guns, for firing heavy projectiles at a high angle, dropping almost vertically in enemy trenches.
FIND. THE KING OF ITALY

HOW WE BEAT BACK THE HUNS.

ARMOURED CAR.
Are playing a big part in our offensive, and will stand anything except a direct hit by a high explosive.
FIND. KING GEORGE

HOW WE BEAT BACK THE HUNS

LEWIS MACHINE GUN.
Carries a disc with its ammunition arranged around the edge, firing as it revolves. Used in the field and favoured by the airmen. It fires in any position.
FIND. PRESIDENT POINCARÉ

Gellert, Die Hölle am Isonzo 4.
Innerkofler, von einer Kugel getroffen, stürzte in die Tiefe.

160   BRITAIN 1915-16   Souvenir cards

161   BERLIN 1917   Children's book illustration

THE SECRET BATTLEPLANE
PERCY F. WESTERMAN

Ff FRANCE

fu-si-li-er-ma-rin   Le ma-re-chal French

G g GRANDE-BRETAGNE

ga-ri-bal-di-en oc-to-bre 1914 mai 1915   gur-Kha (in-di-en)   gre-na-de et gre-na-di-er

162   BRITAIN 1915

163   FRANCE c1916   Children's book illustration

Imperial War Museum

INVOCANDO IL DIO DELLA VITTORIA

164 ITALY c1917 Postcard
Praying to the God of Victory

Patron: H.M. QUEEN ALEXANDRA.

Telephone:
HOLBORN 5229.

Telegrams:
"AVICULTURE, LONDON."

THE

National Egg Collection for the Wounded

WITH "THE APPROVAL AND GRATEFUL APPRECIATION OF THE WAR OFFICE."

Executive Committee:—

Chairman: HORACE G. HOLMES, ESQ., J.P., F.C.A.   Vice-Chairman: REV. HUGH C. WALLACE
BRIG.-GENERAL A. R. CROPTON ATKINS, C.M.G. (Director of Supplies, War Office).
(Representative: Major R. V. RUSSELL.)
Honorary Director: F. CARL ("Poultry World").

W. H. COOK (Orpington)	H. HESFORD	H. WALKER, J.P.
G. TYRWHITT DRAKE, J.P.	H. E. IVATTS (U.P.C.)	T. WANT, (Poultry Keeping)
F.Z.S. M.B.O.U. (Poultry Club)	H. MORRIS PARRY	Hon. Sec.: R. J. DARTNALL
DR. S. E. DUNKIN	H. FABIAN RUSSELL	Organising Sec.: GAMBIER BOLTON

154, FLEET STREET, LONDON, E.C. 4.

JCP/PMJ.
Dear Sir (or Madam),

If this unfortunate War, with all its attendant carnage and horrors, was being waged within a few miles of your district and a wounded soldier stricken in the fray was brought to your home, I am sure there is absolutely nothing you would not do in order to immediately take steps to take care of him, and provide for him all the nourishment necessary to his rapid recovery.

Most of us in this country have been spared all the ghastly horrors of war, and we are unable to realise just what war actually is. We cannot be brought face to face with the men who have been wounded, but the wounded men exist in very large numbers, more especially at the large Base Hospitals in France. I would like you to picture in your mind's eye these brave fellows being brought down on stretchers from the trenches to the clearing stations, and from the clearing stations to the Hospitals.

The aim of the National Egg Collection is to ensure that each sick and wounded soldier and sailor shall have the needful supply of new laid eggs to assist him to recovery. Will you help? At the present time our supplies are lamentably short. We must have eggs, more eggs, and yet more eggs, and when the birds are beginning to lay it is pathetic to think so many eggs are going on to the market for ordinary consumption, and that our wounded lads are short.

A list of our Receiving Depots will be furnished on receipt of a postcard; or if none of those are convenient for you we will supply boxes to enable the eggs to travel to us under special pre-paid labels.

If you are unable to send us eggs will you please send us a cash donation? Everybody can help in some possible way.

The wounded must not be short of eggs. I know I shall not appeal to you in vain, and I look forward confidently to hearing from you at an early date.

Yours very truly,

F. Carl

Hon. Director.

165 BRITAIN c1916 Circular

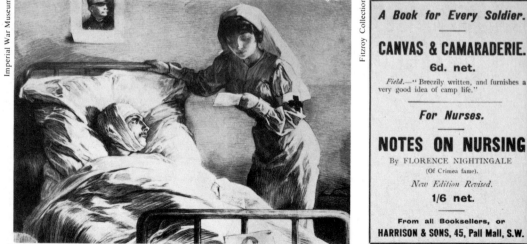

166 FRANCE 1915 Patriotic print   The Sublime Ones

167 BRITAIN 1914 Press ad

DR. BARNARDO'S HOMES

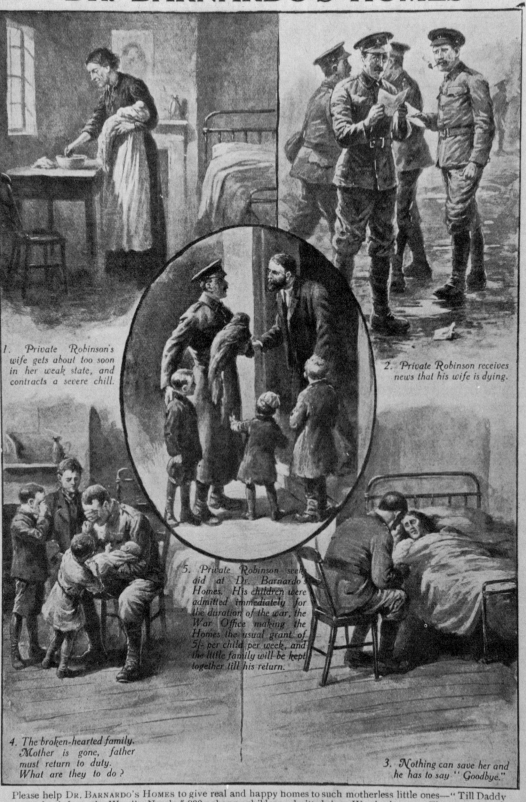

1. Private Robinson's wife gets about too soon in her weak state, and contracts a severe chill.

2. Private Robinson receives news that his wife is dying.

5. Private Robinson seek aid at Dr. Barnardo's Homes. His children were admitted immediately for the duration of the war, the War Office making the Homes the usual grant of 5/- per child per week, and the little family will be kept together till his return.

4. The broken-hearted family. Mother is gone, father must return to duty. What are they to do?

3. Nothing can save her and he has to say "Goodbye."

Please help DR. BARNARDO'S HOMES to give real and happy homes to such motherless little ones—" Till Daddy comes back from the War." Nearly 5,000 unhappy children admitted since War broke out. The cost of Food is very high for a Family always numbering over 7,000 Children. Cheques and Orders, payable " Dr. Barnardo's Homes Food Bill Fund " and crossed (Notes should be Registered), may be addressed to the Honorary Director, WILLIAM BAKER, M.A., LL.B., 18 to 26 STEPNEY CAUSEWAY, LONDON, E.1.

Fitzroy Collection

170   BRITAIN December 1917   Christmas card

A WOMAN'S PART

Imperial War Museum

OFFICIAL COLLECTOR · RUSSIAN · FLAG · DAY · 1917

171   BRITAIN 1917
Flag seller's badge

Imperial War Museum

ASSOCIATION DES DAMES FRANÇAISES

ASSOCIATION DES DAMES FRANÇAISES

CROIX ROUGE FRANÇAISE

PRIX 1ᶠ

20 TIMBRES   1ᵉ SÉRIE, 2ᵐᵉ ÉDITION

a l'Effigie des Grands Chefs de l'Armée Française

Association of Frenchwomen: French Red Cross; 20 stamps showing the great Commanders of the French Army

172   FRANCE c1915   Charity stamp booklet

Imperial War Museum

PLENTY OF BUTTONS

Do not slack up in your work because of temporary shortage of Liberty Bond Buttons. An ample supply is on the way. We are having an emergency quantity manufactured in various plants and are now shipping them as fast as received. In addition a huge supply is in transit from Washington and should be in hand within a few days.

There will be buttons for everybody who buys a bond—and you will not have to wait.

173   UNITED STATES 1918   Promotion announcement

Unnecessary travelling uses Coal required to warm your homes

Keep the home fires burning Low then British Coal will win the war

Less Coal for trains at home means more ships to bring Americans

174   BRITAIN 1917-18   Window cards

Imperial War Museum

From the
Chancellor of The Exchequer
to YOU.

The Food to which these Ration Books relate is available for you only because the British Fleet guards our transport of food from the distant shores where it is produced. To keep the ocean highways open—to protect food-ships that must come in their thousands if we are to live and win—the Navy must be maintained and sustained.

And to win the military victory that must come before peace is possible, the Army and the Royal Air Force must be kept at full strength—provided generously with the weapons and engines of defence and offence.

For these purposes your country needs you to lend your money—not to give it—only to lend it on very profitable terms. This is the duty required of every man and woman here at home—of all of us who, by age or physical weakness or the nature of our work, are held back from actual service with the Colours.

Six things we can do—and should do if we would be worthy of the sacrifices brave men are making for us.

(1) Lives must be lived more simply.

(2) Personal, household and business expenses must be reduced to the minimum.

(3) The surplus of weekly or monthly earnings over necessary expenditure must be invested straightway in National War Bonds or War Savings Certificates.

(4) Current balances at the bank should be kept as small as possible, and the money invested in National War Bonds as and when it comes in.

(5) Private individuals with money on deposit in banks should withdraw as much as they can and invest it in National War Bonds.

(6) Business people and firms with money on deposit should withdraw all not absolutely needed for their business operations and invest it in National War Bonds.

The whole nation is, I am convinced, more determined now than at any time since the struggle began that the War must end in a victorious Peace. To secure this victory, our people do not hesitate to risk, and indeed to give, their own lives and the lives of those dear to them; they will not hesitate to lend their money.

3447. Wt. 21,444/2734. 3,000,000(30). 8/18. S.O.,F.Rd.

175   BRITAIN August 1918   Ration book enclosure

LIKE A WALL OF STEEL—our courageous troops stand in the East and West, protecting our beloved Fatherland against the hordes of the enemy. They seek to destroy us by fire and sword, to submit our women and children to death by starvation.

THINK OF EAST PRUSSIA AND GALICIA! More than three hundred thousand houses burnt and destroyed, many hundreds of thousands of inhabitants deprived of their homesteads and turned out in misery; thousands dragged off and murdered. . . .

NEW ENEMIES, NEW MERCENARIES are being brought in to annihilate everything German from the face of the earth. They hate German fidelity, the German spirit, German endurance. Now, as never before, the call is on us! They must be made to realize what Germans are made of, both at the Front and at Home. . . .

HINDENBURG SHARPENS THE SWORD AFRESH, let us at home show that we are worthy of him. It is our duty cheerfully to supply all that the Fatherland needs to maintain the striking power of our Army and Navy and to ease the burden of our gallant warriors.

OUR WEAPON AT HOME IS THE WAR LOAN. Every German must subscribe. Do not merely subscribe what you happen to have now; covenant what you can spare in the coming months . . . The greater the amount covenanted, that much greater is the effect on our foes and that much nearer is Peace.

GOD IS CLEARLY WITH US. . . . He has blessed our harvest. We shall not starve. German labour and German spirit have struck this contemptible weapon from the hands of our foes. . . . Each of us must do his bit; many are earning more now than in peacetime.

IS IT NOT A SIN to conceal these extra earnings in our time of trial—to fritter them on needless spending, on clothes, luxuries and high living while in the Field our husbands, brothers and sons bear the heaviest of burdens for us all? For every German the greatest economy is the holiest duty. This war will be fought not only with blood and iron but with bread and money. . . .

Everybody must subscribe as much as he can. . . . Subscriptions accepted at all banks, etc etc. . . .

We risk our lives to bring you food.
It's up to you not to waste it.

"A Message from our Seamen"

176   BRITAIN 1917   Poster

Wie eine Mauer von Erz

stehen unsere tapferen, heldenmütigen Truppen in Oft und Weft und schützen unser geliebtes Vaterland vor dem Einbruch der feindlichen Horden. Diese wollen uns mit Feuer und Schwert vernichten, unsere Frauen und Kinder wollen sie dem Hungertode preisgeben.

Denkt an Ostpreußen und Galizien! Über dreihunderttausend

Häuser wurden verbrannt und vernichtet, viele Hunderttausende von Einwohnern verloren Haus und Hof und mußten ins Elend ziehen, tausende wurden weggeschleppt und ermordet.

Neue Feinde, neue Söldlinge hetzen sie in den Vernichtungskrieg,

um alles, was deutsch ist, vom Erdboden zu vertilgen. Sie hassen deutsche Treue, deutschen Geist, deutsche Ausdauer. Jetzt erst recht muß es bei uns heißen! Sie sollen spüren, was der Deutsche vermag draußen im Felde und in der Heimat. Unser

Hindenburg schärft das deutsche Schwert von neuem,

zeigen wir uns daheim seiner würdig. Unsere Pflicht ist es, freudigen Herzens die Mittel zu gewähren, deren das Vaterland zur Aufrechterhaltung der Schlagkraft von Heer und Flotte und zur Erleichterung des Lebens unserer tapferen Krieger bedarf.

Unsere Waffe daheim ist die Kriegsanleihe. Jeder Deutsche

muß zeichnen! Zeichnet nicht nur, was Ihr liegen habt, sondern auch was Ihr in den nächsten Monaten noch erübrigen könnt, denn das Geld braucht nicht sofort eingezahlt werden. Nur der Betrag ist sofort zu zeichnen. Je größer der gezeichnete Betrag ist, um so größer der Eindruck auf unsere Feinde, um so näher der Friede.

Gott ist sichtbar mit uns. Mit reicherer Frucht als wir zu hoffen wagten

hat er unsere Ernte gesegnet. Wir werden nicht verhungern! Deutsche Arbeit, deutscher Geist hat dem Gegner seine niederträchtigen Waffen aus der Hand gewunden. Jeder findet sein Auskommen, sehr viele erzielen viel höheren Verdienst als im Frieden.

Ist es da nicht eine Sünde in dieser schweren Zeit diesen Verdienst

zu verstecken und dem Vaterlande vorzuenthalten oder für unnötige Ausgaben, für Näschereien, Kleider, Luxus und Wohlleben, zu verwenden, während draußen unsere Männer, Brüder und Söhne das Schwerste ertragen — für uns?!

Größte Sparsamkeit ist heiligste Pflicht jedes Deutschen.

Dieser Krieg wird nicht nur mit Blut und Eisen geführt, sondern auch mit Brot und Geld.

Des Deutschen Kriegssparkasse ist die Kriegsanleihe

Wenn draußen unsere heldenhaften Truppen die feindlichen tod- und verderbenbringenden Feuerschlünde stürmen, dann müssen sie wissen, daß auch zu Hause jeder, soweit es in seiner Kraft steht, mithilft zum Sieg und Frieden.

Darum zeichne jeder Kriegsanleihe,

niemand darf sich ausschließen — jeder zeichne, soviel er kann.

Zeichnungen nehmen alle Banken, Sparkassen, Lebensversicherungsgesellschaften, Kreditgenossenschaften, sowie Postanstalten entgegen und geben gern Auskunft.

BERNHARD

177   GERMANY 1916   Poster

178   GERMANY 1917   Poster

CITY OF FRANKFURT: VOUCHER This voucher will be encashed by the main City Bank of Frankfurt. The date when validity expires will be publicly announced—The Magistrate, Frankfurt am Main.

179   FRANKFURT, GERMANY May 1917

WILLS'S "SEA KING" PLUG

5^d Per Plug.   5^d Per Plug.

W. D & H. O. Wills,
London & Bristol

180   BRITAIN c1914   Showcard

YMCA

Arguments Against

the use of

Obscene Language

RED TRIANGLE PUBLICATION No. 15

Don't Use Language Your Mother Would Blush to Hear

The use of Obscene Language should be absolutely suppressed for the following reasons:

1. IMPURE WORDS give rise to impure thoughts. The result is a polluted mind and a perverted imagination.

2. A PERVERTED IMAGINATION destroys character, and, if unchecked, may eventually destroy life itself through venereal disease.

3. SMUTTY JOKES appeal to the brute nature; they grate on the finer sensibilities of true men. A GENTLEMEN never tells a yarn, or listens to one that he would not care his mother or sisters to hear.

4. FILTHY TALK reveals an obscene mind, and insults the person who hears it.

5. OBSCENITY is generally a sign of ignorance; there are plenty of decent words in the English language to adequately express every shade of meaning.

181   UNITED STATES 1918   Leaflet

182   GERMANY 1914   Playing cards

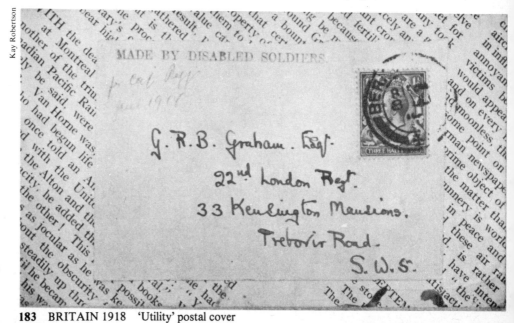

MADE BY DISABLED SOLDIERS.

G. R. B. Graham. Esq.
22nd London Regt.
33 Kensington Mansions.
Trebovir Road.
S. W. 5.

183   BRITAIN 1918   'Utility' postal cover

185 BRITAIN c1917
Charity flag

186 BRITAIN c1917
Charity flag

184 GERMANY/AUSTRIA
1915-16   Charity ribbons

(Left) Long live the Defenders of Przemysl

(Centre) Long Live the Rulers of the Victorious
Quadruple Alliance

(Right) Long Live Champneuville, Côte de Talou

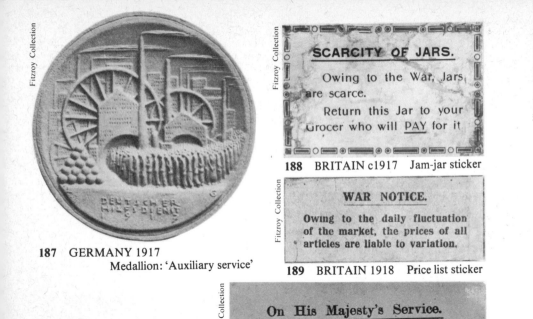

187   GERMANY 1917
Medallion: 'Auxiliary service'

SCARCITY OF JARS.

Owing to the War, Jars
are scarce.

Return this Jar to your
Grocer who will **PAY** for it

188   BRITAIN c1917   Jam-jar sticker

WAR NOTICE.

Owing to the daily fluctuation
of the market, the prices of all
articles are liable to variation.

189   BRITAIN 1918   Price list sticker

On His Majesty's Service.

To the Head of the Household.

190   FRANCE c1918   Poster

THE POTATO SAVED GERMANY! But its
efforts must not flag. Stores of dried potatoes and
starch must free us from the dangers of uncertain
harvests. So plant more potatoes! Increase the yield
by planting best seed potatoes, by seed rotation, by
better fertilizing and good husbandry. Further information from . . . etc etc. . . .

191   GERMANY 1917   Poster

Ministry of Food,
Grosvenor House, W.1.

ON HIS MAJESTY'S SERVICE.

I wish to appeal for the immediate help of every man,
woman and child in my effort to reduce the consumption of
bread.

We must all eat less food; especially we must all eat
less bread and none of it must be wasted. The enemy is
trying to take away our daily bread. He is sinking our
wheat ships. If he succeeds in starving us our soldiers
will have died in vain.

In the interests of the country, I call upon you all
to deny yourselves, and so loyally to bridge over the anxious
days between now and the harvest. Every man must deny himself; every mother, for she is the mistress of the home,
must see that her family makes its own sacrifice and that
not a crust or crumb is wasted.

By a strict care of our daily bread we can best help
the men who are gallantly fighting on sea and land to
achieve victory, and so share with them the joys of the
peace which will follow.

No true citizen, no patriotic man or woman will fail
the country in this hour of need.

I ask all the members of your household to pledge
themselves to respond to the King's recent Appeal for
economy and frugality and to wear the purple ribbon as a
token.

29th May, 1917.

Food Controller.

192   BRITAIN May 1917   Circular

ORDER COAL NOW

UNITED STATES FUEL ADMINISTRATION

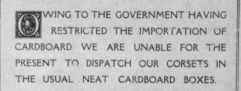

194   BRITAIN c1917   Package enclosure

AVIS
DÉCLARATION des POULES & COQS

Les propriétaires de poules et coqs sont informés qu'ils ont à faire connaître à leur Mairie respective et avant le 18 Janvier 1918:

1° Le nombre de poules âgées de moins de 9 mois;

2° Le nombre de poules âgées de 9 mois à 3 ans;

3° Le nombre de poules âgées de plus de 3 ans;

4° Le nombre de coqs.

Les propriétaires de volailles désignées ci-dessus qui ne se soumettraient pas à cet ordre verront leurs volailles confisquées et une amende de 500 marks sera infligée par poule non déclarées.

Croix-Wasquehal, le 11 Janvier 1918.

ORTSKOMMANDANTUR CROIX-WASQUEHAL,
I. V.
SOMMERFELDT,
Hauptmann.

N°

Pour Croix, les déclarations seront faites à la Mairie, 1° étage, 1° guichet.

195   CROIX, FRANCE January 1918   Notice

HEN AND COCKEREL CENSUS Owners of hens and cockerels are informed that they are to make known to their respective municipal offices before January 18, 1918 (1) The number of hens aged under 9 months; (2) the number of hens between 9 months and 3 years; (3) the number of hens over 3 years, and (4) the number of cockerels. Owners of poultry as above who fail to comply with this order will have their birds confiscated and will be fined 500 marks for each bird not declared.—Sommerfeldt, Regional Commander, Croix-Wasquehal

3   UNITED STATES 1918   Poster

Save Food

U. S. FOOD ADMINISTRATION

US 1918   Window sticker

The Dollar Watch now $1.35

European war conditions have boosted copper, the principal material in watch construction, from 13.73c. per pound in July, 1914, to 37.5c. per pound in March, 1917. It threatens to go still higher. Labor costs more not only directly, but indirectly, on account of the smaller output due to unsettled conditions. Everything used in watch making, from acids to watch brass, has increased from 35 per cent to 300 per cent. We would not sacrifice the widely established reputation of the Ingersoll "Dollar Watch" by lowering its quality. To maintain quality the price had to be raised. As soon as conditions are normal again, the old price will be restored.

ROBT. H. INGERSOLL & BRO.

197   UNITED STATES April 1917   Press advertisement

Kriegsgefangenensendung.

TO.

Ref. P. M. Bartlett

Christ Church

Faraday Road

Notting Hill

London

England.

Dr Sir

I am Writing these few lines to
let you no that I am a Prisoner of War
I should be very Please if you could
Assist me in any small way of a
Parcel of Foodstuff.

Yours Truly R A Easdon

22/12/15

camp in which interned with Barrack and group etc. Enclosed label(s)
must be used only for packages exceeding 11.lbs. in weight. All the
particulars indicated on the label should be entered in the spaces
provided for the purpose. As a safeguard against the label becoming
detached, this information and the address should be marked on the
package(s) independently of the label.

Parcels should be carefully packed in several sheets of stout
paper and firmly tied, and an extra length of string, and an additional
sheet of paper, with address, should be placed inside the parcel for
use in case it is opened at the Customs House and has to be retied.

Articles of food should be packed in wooden boxes. Fresh fruit and
meat cannot be sent. Bread should be packed as advised in enclosed note
before placing in the box. The use of tins must be restricted as far
as possible.

Arrangements have been made by the Prisoners of War Help Committee
with the American Express Co. for the transportation of packages
exceeding 11.lbs. in weight and such packages should be forwarded to the
American Express Co. 6 Haymarket, London, S.W. For this purpose the
labels must be employed.

There will be no charge for transport. Provided the enclosed label
is used, parcels will be received at any Railway Parcel Office and
will be forwarded to London and then to Germany free of charge.

On no account should letters or newspapers be enclosed in parcels,
and failure to observe this will result in parcel being confiscated.
Newspapers should not be used for packing.

While every effort will be made to ensure delivery, the Committee
cannot, in view of existing conditions, assume any liability in the
event of packages failing to reach consignees, and it must be clearly
understood that they will be accepted for transmission at owners own risk.

A receipt will be sent from London for all parcels dispatched. Should
such receipt not reach the sender promptly the attention of the Committee
should be drawn to the fact by letter stating address on package, when

198 GERMANY December 1915 British PoW message card   **199** BRITAIN c1915 Circular

Donor's Name and Address.

Name und Wohnort des
Gebers.

Coldstream Guards Prisoners Fund
Mr. Christie Miller,
81, St. James' Place,
London, S.W.

Kriegsgefangenensendung.

Packed and despatched by "COLDSTREAM GUARDS' PRISONERS
OF WAR FUND," under authority granted by the Central Prisoners of
War Committee of the British Red Cross Society and the Order of St.
John of Jerusalem in England.

Verpackt und versendet mit der Autorisierung des Central-Komitee für Kriegsgefangene
des Britischen Roten Kreuzes und der Vereinigung St. Johannes von Jerusalem
in England.

CONTENTS. INHALT.

Parcel No. and Date of Despatch No. 2 Dec 12th

BRITISCHER KRIEGSGEFANGENER.

Food Comforts
Special Mince
Towels.
Handkerchiefs

8395.

Alsopp. C.E. pte

Komp. 4.

Engländer Koim: 2,

Friedrichsfeld

GERMANY.

200 TARBES, FRANCE 1916
Prisoner of War charity medallion   **201** BRITAIN 1918 (?) Prisoner of War parcel label

Telephone No. MAYFAIR 4395.

Russian Prisoners of War Help Committee.

President:
THE COUNTESS BENCKENDORFF.

Chairman of Executive Committee:
THE EARL OF DERBY, K.G.

Hon. Treasurer:
THE LORD REVELSTOKE, G.C.V.O.

Hon. Secretary:
Professor SIR PAUL VINOGRADOFF.

Secretary:
G. D. JEFFERSON.

18, GLOUCESTER PLACE,

PORTMAN SQUARE,

LONDON, W. 1

2nd January, 1918.

The Russian Prisoners of War Help Committee begs to inform you that in view of the recent developments it finds it necessary to close its operations for the Russian Prisoners.

The Committee greatly regrets that it will be impossible to send parcels to the Russian Soldiers, Prisoners of War, in enemy countries from and after the 15th January, 1918.

The Committee would take this opportunity to express to you their sincere thanks and warm appreciation for all that you have done for the Russians in captivity, who being most grateful for your kindness will bear it in lasting remembrance.

18, GLOUCESTER PLACE, W.

202 BRITAIN January 1918 Circular

SANITAS
Domestic Soap
Specially packed
for distribution to
Prisoners of War.

The "Sanitas" Co., Ltd.,
Limehouse, London, E.

Fitzroy Collection

203 BRITAIN 1917 (?)
Prisoner of War soap wrapper

People's Fund for German
War and Civilian Internees

Volksspende
für die deutschen
Kriegs- und Zivil
Gefangenen

204 GERMANY 1918 Poster

CLOTHING FOR PRISONERS OF WAR Prisoners need warm clothing. . . . Many, captive since summer, are totally unprovided. . . . Civilians too, taken in the clothes they stood up in in the invaded areas . . . need clothes. . . . Gifts, in cash or kind, gratefully received. . . .

LE VÊTEMENT DU PRISONNIER DE GUERRE

RATTACHÉ A LA ✚ FRANÇAISE

63, Avenue des Champs-Elysées, PARIS

Victoria and Albert Museum

205 FRANCE 1915 Poster

KENTISH FLAG DAY
IN AID OF OUR
KENTISH
PRISONERS
IN
Germany.
MONDAY, AUG. 2nd.
Please All Help.

All willing to help as Collectors, apply to Mrs.
Goold, The Nest, Knight's Avenue; or Mrs. Hugh
Raven, Bartield House, Broadstairs.

Fitzroy Collection

206 BRITAIN c1917 Leaflet

HOTEL · RESTAURANT · PENSION
ZÄHRINGERHOF
HALLER-STRASSE — A. KERN=BURGER · BERN — LANG-GASSE
TELEPHON Nr. 112 :: TELEGRAMME: ZÄHRINGERHOF BERN
5 MINUTEN VOM BAHNHOF :: TRAM Nr. 5 :: HALTSTELLE HALLERSTRASSE
PORTIER AM BAHNHOF

KOMFORTABLE ZIMMER VON FR. 2.– AN | BILLARD EIGENE MUSIK · TÄGLICH
TABLE D'HOTE RESTAURATION | KONZERTE · AUSGEZ. BIER · REELLE OFFENE
A LA CARTE ZU JEDER TAGESZEIT | UND fl. FLASCHENWEINE · SPEZIALITÄTEN IN
· LOKALE FÜR VEREINE, HOCHZEITEN ETC. · | KELLER UND KÜCHE · ZIMMER MIT PENSION
PRIX MODÉRES

BERN, den Aug 1st 1917

Dear Hon Sec

Just a few lines thanking you for the parcels I received from you while I was in Germany & to let you know that I shall not require any more as I have escaped from Germany. I ran away from work at 4-0 pm July 27th, swam across the river Rhine & landed in Switzerland about 12-30 am July 30th. I am now in Berne & have to remain here a few days at least. I hope to return to England shortly

8617 H Wilson Act Cpl
1st Batta Coldstream Guards

Coldstream Guards Prisoners Fund
Mrs. Christie Miller,
21, St. James' Place,
London, S.W.

LE LANGAGE SECRET
A l'Usage des Prisonniers de Guerre

EXEMPLE :

Description :

La rigueur de la surveillance obligera souvent nos pauvres prisonniers au silence et par conséquent les forcera à se communiquer des secrets par signes, par exemple l'arrivée d'un nouveau, revenant du front, pourra les initier à ce langage et les mettre au courant des ...

SECRET LANGUAGE for Prisoners of War. Close surveillance will often force our poor prisoners to silence, and consequently to communication by secret signs. . . . This new language may be used . . . even in darkness or by deaf-mutes or the blind . . . and movements are so slight as to arouse no suspicion. Each phalange represents a letter. It is very easy to learn. . . . All that is needed is to stick numbered and lettered pieces of paper to the fingers. . . .

207   FRANCE c1916   Postcard   **208   BERNE, SWITZERLAND August 1917   Letter**

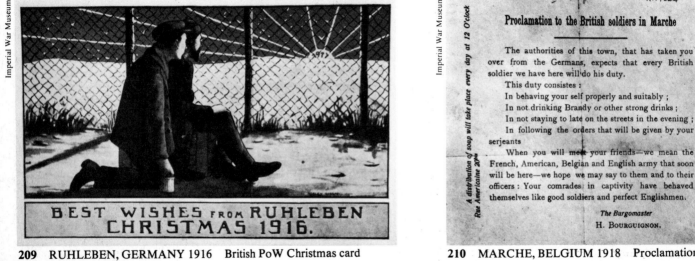

BEST WISHES FROM RUHLEBEN
CHRISTMAS 1916.

209   RUHLEBEN, GERMANY 1916   British PoW Christmas card

R.17/344

Proclamation to the British soldiers in Marche

The authorities of this town, that has taken you over from the Germans, expects that every British soldier we have here will do his duty.

This duty consistes :

In behaving your self properly and suitably ;

In not drinking Brandy or other strong drinks ;

In not staying to late on the streets in the evening ;

In following the orders that will be given by your serjeants

When you will meet your friends—we mean the French, American, Belgian and English army that soon will be here—we hope we may say to them and to their officers : Your comrades in captivity have behaved themselves like good soldiers and perfect Englishmen.

The Burgomaster
H. BOURGUIGNON.

A distribution of soap will take place every day at 12 O'clock
Rue Americaine 20bis

210   MARCHE, BELGIUM 1918   Proclamation

211   ISLE OF MAN 1914 PoW magazine cover

BUCKINGHAM PALACE

1918.

The Queen joins me in welcoming you on your release from the miseries & hardships, which you have endured with so much patience & courage.

During these many months of trial, the early rescue of our gallant Officers & Men from the cruelties of their captivity has been uppermost in our thoughts.

We are thankful that this longed for day has arrived, & that back in the old Country you will be able once more to enjoy the happiness of a home & to see good days among those who anxiously look for your return.

George R.I.

213   LONDON 1918   Letter

To the (PoW camp) Commandant: We respectfully beg to ask the Commandant to grant the following requests: (1) To order all letters actually in Camp to be delivered daily. (2) According to the orders of the Camp Sergeant, no clothing, books, etc., are to be placed in the recesses adjoining the beds. We request that a suitable place be assigned to us for the depositing of articles, as our boxes are removed as soon as their contents are withdrawn. (3) For the sake of our health we beg to be allowed the means of preserving in good condition our provisions in the cardboard packets and boxes.

212   WOODFORD   July 1918   PoW letter

214   GERMANY 1918 PoW currency

Situation April 21st 1918. Secret

DIVISIONS WITHDRAWN			DIVISIONS IN RESERVE IN ARMIES				DIVISIONS IN LINE	
			Proven	59	(8211)	YPRES	36	(7111)
			Poperinghe	79	(7372)		41	(3110)
	40	6176		25	(8014)		6	(5044)
				34	(6783)	WYTSCHAETE	21	(4999)
			Brandhoek	49	(2972)		39	(3983)
	66	5869					30	(4580)
			Hondeghem	29	(4019)		9	(6285)
			Staple	38	(2437)	BAILLEUL	1A	(410)
							31	(5800)
			La Motte	2 Cav.	(1672)	MERVILLE	5	(800)
Roquetoire	50	(8492)	Estree Blanche	1 Cav.	(765)		61	(6488)
			Aire	16	(5874)		4	(2499)
			Lillers	14	(5789)	BETHUNE	3	(4333)
			St Hilaire	31	(6343)		1	(1538)
			Cauchy a la Tour	3 Cav.	(523)		11	(824)
			Auchel	55	(2567)	LENS	3c	(189)
			Barlin	46	(176)		4c	(329)
			Valhoun	24	3936		1c	(163)
			Monchy Breton	20	5690	R. SCARPE	15	(1979)
							56	(1425)
Brailly	47	(3526)	Bavincourt	Guards	(1178)		2c	(208)
							2	(2403)
			Pos.	57	(150)	AYETTE	32	(573)
			Authies	37	(950)		62	(1664)
			Rainchevol	63	(3091)		42	(2044)
			Toutencourt	12	(2289)	HEBUTERNE	N.Z.	(1470)
							17	(2118)
							35	(2986)
						ALBERT	38	(232)
			Allonville	4A	(1273)		2A	(467)
						R. SOMME	3A	(569)
							5A	(425)
							8	(4467)
			Cavillon	18	(4646)		58	2693

CASUALTIES OF INFANTRY AND CAVALRY INCURRED SINCE MARCH 21st '18, AND REPORTED UP TO APRIL 21st '18 SHOWN IN BRACKETS.

DIVISIONS SHOWN IN RED HAVE HAD OVER 3,500 CASUALTIES.

◯ DENOTES DIVISIONS NOT BEING MADE UP OWING TO LACK OF REINFORCEMENTS.

FRENCH AND PORTUGUESE DIVISIONS ARE NOT INCLUDED.

216 FRANCE April 1918   Casualty list

215   PARIS August 1914
Casualty list

Morts au champ d'honneur

Nous apprenons la mort de :

Le colonel Prat, de l'infanterie territoriale, tué à l'ennemi.

Le lieutenant-colonel Heude, du 1er zouaves, décédé à Nogent-sur-Marne des suites de ses blessures.

Le lieutenant-colonel Delagrange, du 251e d'infanterie, tué le 25 août dans le Nord, en menant la charge de son régiment.

Le lieutenant-colonel de Hauteclocque, du 11e hussards, tué en Belgique.

Le lieutenant-colonel Dubujadoux, directeur du cabinet militaire du gouverneur de l'Algérie, tué le 7 septembre à la tête du 2e régiment de marche des zouaves.

Le lieutenant-colonel Angelvy du 22e d'infanterie, tué à l'ennemi.

Le capitaine Mourey, du 2e colonial, tué à l'ennemi.

Le capitaine Pierre Robin, fils du directeur honoraire de la Banque de France, tué à Fère-Champenoise.

Le lieutenant Jean Marot, du 314e, fils du président de la Chambre de commerce des Deux-Sèvres, tué en Lorraine.

L'abbé Kupperschmitt, sergent au 209e, tué à l'ennemi.

L'abbé Marcel Baniol, vicaire à Avignon, sergent d'infanterie coloniale, tué à l'ennemi.

Le caporal Henri Brugère, neveu du général, tué à l'ennemi.

Le capitaine Deremetz, du 11e dragons, tué à Altkirch.

Le capitaine Sabouret, du 40e d'artillerie, décédé à Rouen des suites de ses blessures.

Le capitaine Gabriel de Villedon de Courson, du 4e colonial, décédé des suites de ses blessures à l'hôpital de Laval.

Le lieutenant Francis Lecoq, fils de l'ancien bâtonnier de Clermont-Ferrand, tué au combat de Pommiers (Aisne).

Le commandant Schwaeblé, du 277e d'infanterie, chef du bureau de la préparation militaire au ministère de la guerre, tué le 20 août en Alsace, cité à l'ordre du jour de l'armée.

M. Henri Lacointe, sergent au 228e d'infanterie, mort de ses blessures le 18 septembre, à l'hôpital auxiliaire du territoire, 19, rue Crillon.

Le lieutenant Roth, de l'artillerie, frère du préfet du Morbihan, tué le 7 septembre à la bataille de Fère-Champenoise.

NOS BLESSÉS

Marseille. — Un train sanitaire a

THE ROLL OF HONOUR.

TOTAL CASUALTIES LITTLE MORE THAN 32,000.

690 Missing Munsters.

And how can man die better
Than facing fearful odds,
For the ashes of his fathers
And the temples of his gods?
—Macaulay.

Although for several weeks no approximate returns have been issued by the War Office of British casualties in France, a fairly correct estimate can be formed by adding the totals contained in the two despatches from Sir John French. There is

WOUNDED AND PRISONERS.

Button, Sec. Lieut. G. T., Ox. and Bucks L.I.
Doughty, Major E. C. Suffolk Regt.
French, Lieut. C. T. T. O'B., R. Irish Regt.
Godsal, Capt. F., Ox. and Bucks L.I.
Morley, Capt. C., Manchester Regt.
Oxford, Capt. E., Suffolk Regt.
Spencer, Sec. Lieut. E. A., R.F.A.
Thomas, Sec. Lieut. R. W., R. Munster Fus.

N.C.O.'S AND MEN.

KILLED.

Austin, 9726 Pte. F., R. Scots.
Barber, 10403 Corpl. W., R. Scots.
Bartlett, 8514 Pte. F., R. Irish Regt.
Bonner, 8862 Pte. G., R. Scots.
Byrd, 10238 Pte.

217 LONDON September 1914   News cutting (*News of the World*)

218 UNITED STATES May 1918
Antigo Journal cartoon

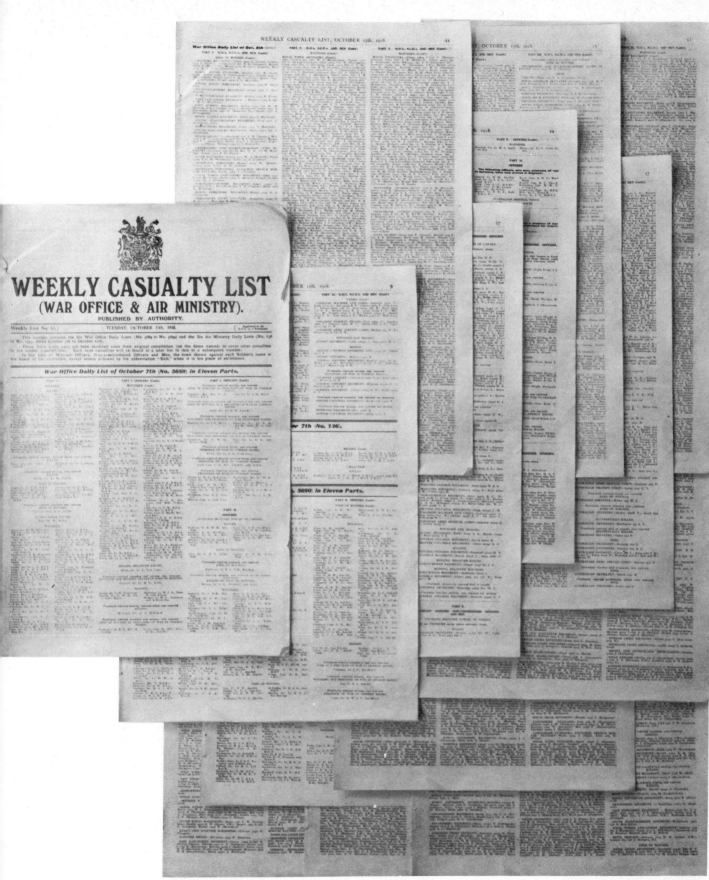

How to carry the Box Respirator and the P.H. Helmet.

1. Carry the Box Respirator slung on the chest as in the "Alert" position, but with the satchel flap buttoned.

2. Carry the P.H. Helmet slung from the left shoulder perpendicularly downwards, the sling passing under the belt.

3. THE BOX RESPIRATOR AND HELMET MUST BE OUTSIDE ALL OTHER EQUIPMENT.

Action to be taken on Gas Alert.

1. Unbutton the Box Respirator satchel but leave the flap in position. If you have no Box Respirator, carry the P.H. Helmet in the "Alert" position.

2. Put the chin strap of the steel helmet at the back of the head so that the helmet can be quickly removed.

3. SEE THAT NOTHING IS SLUNG ACROSS THE CHEST which might interfere with the rapid putting on of Respirator or Helmet.

Action to be taken on Gas Alarm.

1. IMMEDIATELY put on your Box Respirator. If you have no Box Respirator, put on your Helmet.

2. Rouse all men in the trenches, etc., and warn all employed men.

3. Let down the blanket curtains of protected shelters and fix them in position.

4. Stand to arms.

Action to be taken during a Gas Attack.

1. Do not move to a flank or to the rear. Do not go into any dug-out unless you are wearing a Respirator or Helmet.

2. MOVE ABOUT AS LITTLE AS POSSIBLE. TALK ONLY WHEN ABSOLUTELY NECESSARY.

3. Look out to help men who may be wounded, or whose Box Respirators or Helmets may have been damaged.

4. If your Box Respirator is damaged and you have to change to the Helmet, HOLD YOUR BREATH until the change is effected.

Action to be taken after a Gas Attack.

1. DO NOT TAKE OFF YOUR MASK OR HELMET UNTIL ORDERED TO DO SO.

2. Clean and dry your Respirator Mask and treat the eyepieces with anti-dimming composition.

3. REPLACE YOUR BOX RESPIRATOR OR HELMET IN THE "ALERT" POSITION AND BE PREPARED FOR ANOTHER ATTACK.

4. DO NOT GO INTO ANY SHELTER UNTIL IT HAS BEEN VENTILATED BY FIRES OR FANNING unless you are wearing a Respirator or Helmet.

5. Clean your arms and ammunition and re-oil them.

For points to be observed when inspecting Anti-Gas Appliances.—See p. 4 over.

220 BRITAIN March 1917 Gas defence instruction card

■ Während des Gasangriffes. Originalzeichnung von Edmund Cezt ■

221 GERMANY c1915 Magazine illustration: *During the Gas attack*

... the lung, and it occurs ch... in the... and second day after exposure to Phosgene. A few cases may chance to develop secondary bacterial infections of the lungs and to succumb to a later broncho-pneumonia, but they are relatively rare.

The main clinical features of acute Phosgene poisoning may therefore be summarized as follows:

(i) Catching of the breath, choking, and coughing *immediately* on exposure to the gas.

(ii) Inability to expand the chest in a full breath after removal from the poisoned air.

(iii) Vomiting, hurried shallow respiration, and sometimes coughing with an abundant expectoration, follow. Pain is felt behind the sternum and across the lower part of the chest. Fine râles are heard in the axillae and over the back.

(iv) Cyanosis next appears, in association either with a full venous congestion or with the pallid face of circulatory failure. The development of these dangerous symptoms may occur after many hours' delay, and sometimes with unexpected rapidity in an apparently slight case as the result of muscular effort.

(v) Death, which may or may not be preceded by mild delirium or unconsciousness, rarely occurs after the first or second day.

Di-chlor-ethyl-sulphide is spoken of as being a *vesicant*. It may exert its irritant action either as a vapour in low concentration in the air or by direct contact from splashes of the liquid. The liquid or vapour clings to the clothing of men exposed to Yellow Cross shells, and thus slowly exerts its continuously irritant action on their bodies.

No irritant effect at all is felt on first exposure, whatever the concentration may be, but after a delay of about two to six hours the skin and mucous membranes begin to react with a progressive inflammation that may result in local necrosis and desquamation of these covering membranes. There is intense conjunctivitis; the skin turns an angry red, and this erythema is soon followed by skin blistering here and there over the face and body. The passage of the vapour down the respiratory tract may cause such severe injury to the lining mucous membranes of the trachea and bronchioles that they are eventually destroyed and sloughed away. Bacterial infection then seizes upon the raw surfaces, and the

222 BRITAIN 1918 *Atlas of Gas Poisoning*

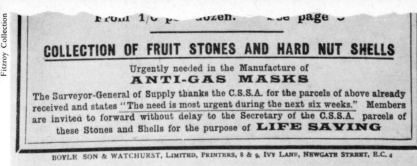

COLLECTION OF FRUIT STONES AND HARD NUT SHELLS

Urgently needed in the Manufacture of
ANTI-GAS MASKS

The Surveyor-General of Supply thanks the C.S.S.A. for the parcels of above already
received and states "The need is most urgent during the next six weeks." Members
are invited to forward without delay to the Secretary of the C.S.S.A. parcels of
these Stones and Shells for the purpose of **LIFE SAVING**

BOYLE SON & WATCHURST, LIMITED, PRINTERS, 8 & 9, IVY LANE, NEWGATE STREET, E.C. 4

223 LONDON October 1918   Portion of provision merchant's leaflet

225 UNITED STATES 1916
Sheet music

224 UNITED STATES 1918   Poster

226 WESTERN FRONT c1917   Notice

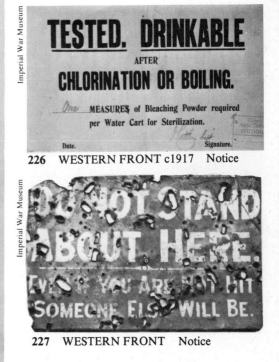

227 WESTERN FRONT   Notice

12 MINOR HORRORS OF WAR

caused much irritation to the skin and disturbed men's sleep.

Lice occur chiefly on the body (*Pediculus vestimenti*) and head (*P. capitis*). They are small greyish-white insects. The female lays about sixty eggs during two weeks; the eggs hatch after nine to ten days. The lice are small at first; they undergo several moults and grow in size, sucking blood every few hours, and attain sexual maturity in about two weeks. The eggs will not develop unless maintained at a temperature of 22° C. or over—such as prevails in clothing worn on the human body or in the hair of the head. This is why, *when clothing is worn continuously*, men are more prone to become infested with lice derived from habitually unclean persons, their clothing, bedding, &c. *P. capitis* lives between the hair in the head, and the eggs, called 'nits,' are attached to the hairs. *P. vestimenti* lives in the clothing, to which it usually remains attached when feeding on man; it lays its eggs in the clothing, and usually retreats into the seams and permanent folds therein. This is of importance in considering the means of destroying lice.

To avoid these pests the following rules should be observed:—

1. Search your person as often as possible for signs of the presence of lice—that is, their

THE LOUSE 13

bites. As soon as these are found, lose no time in taking the measures noted under paragraph 5.

2. Try not to sleep where others, especially the unclean, have slept before. Consider this in choosing a camping-ground.

3. Change your clothing as often as practicable. After clothes have been discarded for a week the lice are usually dead of starvation. Change clothes at night if possible, and place your clothing away from that of others. Jolting of carts in transport aids in spreading the lice, which also become disseminated by crawling about from one kit to another. Infested clothing and blankets, until dealt with, should be kept apart as far as possible.

4. Verminous clothes for which there is no further use should be burnt, buried, or sunk in water.

5. If lice are found on the person, they may be *readily destroyed by the application of either petrol, paraffin oil, turpentine, xylol, or benzine*. Apply these to the head in the case of *P. capitis*. Remember that these fluids are all highly inflammable. When possible, soap and wash the head twenty-four hours after the last application of petrol, &c. The application may be repeated on two or more days if the infestation is heavy. Fine combs are useful

228 BRITAIN 1915 Double-spread from *Minor Horrors of War* A. E. Shipley

229 UNITED STATES 1918 Sheet music

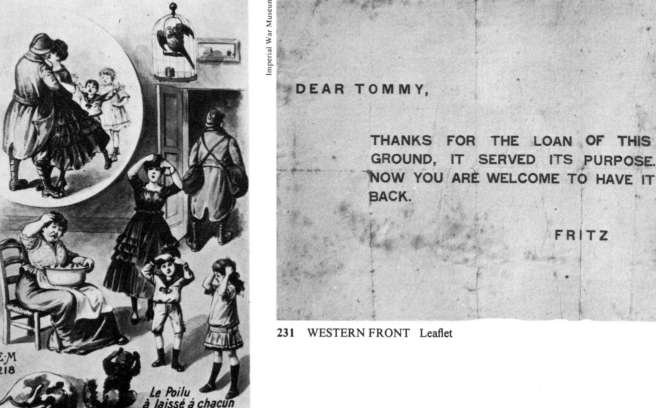

230 FRANCE c1916 Postcard

The poilu has left
to each his
little souvenir

DEAR TOMMY,

THANKS FOR THE LOAN OF THIS GROUND, IT SERVED ITS PURPOSE. NOW YOU ARE WELCOME TO HAVE IT BACK.

FRITZ

231 WESTERN FRONT Leaflet

MESSAGES AND SIGNALS.

No. of Message............

Prefix...A.H....Code......O859.....Words...No...7....	Received.	Sent, or sent out.	Office Stamp
£ s. d.	From...............	At...............m.	
Charges to Collect	By...............	To...............	
Service Instructions.		By...............	

URGENT OPERATION PRIORITY

Handed in at......................Office..........m.   Received..................m.

TO   66ᵗʰ Dⁱᵛ

*Sender's Number	Day of Month	In reply to Number	AAA
G.98	11ᵗʰ		

Hostilities	will	cease	at
11·00	hrs	today Nov 11	troops
will stand	fast	on line	reached at
that hour	which	will be	reported
to Advanced Army		by wire	via
Defensive	precautions	will be	maintained
there will	be no	intercourse of	any
discription	with	the enemy	until
receipt	of instructions	from Army	
H.Q.	aaa.	further	instructions
follow.			

FROM	66 Dⁱᵛ.
TIME & PLACE	

*This line should be erased if not required

C. & R. 7800. Wt. W14832/M1523 100,000. 3/17. (E930). Forms C/2128.

233   BRITAIN November 1918   Facsimile and translation of *Berliner Tageblatt* for November 11 1918, published in London

LIBERATION LOAN We *have* them!
[Wording refers to earlier
slogan: 'On les aura!'—
'We will get them!']

234   LONDON Nov 1918 Poster

235   PARIS Nov 1918 Poster

236   US 1919 Press ad

BEKANNTMACHUNG

Der Bevoelkerung wird folgendes bekannt gegeben:

Die Deutsche Regierung wird an die feindlichen Regierungen das Ersuchen richten, dass der Dreistaedtebezirk LILLE-ROU-BAIX-TOURCOING unter allen Umstaenden von einer Beschiessung ausgenommen wird, damit die Staedte erhalten bleiben und Opfer unter der Bevoelkerung vermieden werden.

K. H. Qu. den 12. Oktober 1918.

AVIS

La population est informée de ce qui suit :

Le Gouvernement Allemand demandera aux Gouvernements ennemis qu'un bombardement du district des trois villes LILLE-ROU-BAIX-TOURCOING soit empêché en toutes circonstances, afin de conserver les villes et d'éviter des victimes parmi la population.

K. H. Qu. le 12-10-1918.

DER KOMMANDIERENDE GENERAL.

237 FRANCE October 1918 Proclamation

**239 BRITAIN November 18 1918
Press advertisement**

BEKANNTMACHUNG

To all Persons in Places entered and occupied by the Forces of His Britannic Majesty:

I WARN ALL PERSONS in this place THAT THEY MUST NOT IMPERIL the safety of any Officer or Man in the service of HIS BRITANNIC MAJESTY OR the operations of HIS BRITANNIC MAJESTY'S FORCES. IT IS the DUTY of all persons to help in the repression of any act which offends against my Orders and I CALL UPON all State and Municipal Officials to help in maintaining good behaviour.

I DECLARE THAT ALL INHABITANTS OF THIS PLACE WILL BE PROTECTED so long as they conduct themselves in an obedient and peaceable manner BUT WITHOUT PREJUDICE TO THE right of HIS BRITANNIC MAJESTY and His Troops to exact such punishment as is recognised by International Law against any place in which this Proclamation is disregarded.

THE MORE READILY OBEDIENCE IS SHOWN TO MY ORDERS THE GREATER WILL BE THE SECURITY OF THE INHABITANTS.

AND I DECLARE THAT:

1. IF VIOLENCE is done to any Officer or Man under my Command, or if any stores, supplies, equipment or other property of the Army under my command are stolen or injured, or
2. IF DAMAGE is done to any building, road, railway, canal, bridge, telegraph, telephone, water supply or other useful works, or to any supplies, or if any such works or supplies are in any way interfered with or rendered unsafe or unsuitable for use.

The persons directly responsible, whether as principals or accessories will, after due trial, be punished with DEATH or such other penalty as I may decree.

AND I ALSO DECLARE THAT THE SEVEREST PENALTIES WILL BE INFLICTED UPON:

1. Any person AIDING, HIDING or otherwise assisting any German or other enemy soldier or anyone who is or has been ACTING IN DISOBEDIENCE OF MY ORDERS.
2. Any person concealing or failing to disclose any MEANS OF COMMUNICATING WITH THE ENEMIES OF HIS BRITANNIC MAJESTY.
3. Any person who does not IMMEDIATELY OBEY EVERY ORDER affecting him or his property, movable and immovable.
4. Any Person doing any act, whether specially prohibited by regulation or not, which may be to the prejudice of good order or endanger the welfare or safety of any of the TROOPS OR SUBJECTS OF HIS BRITANNIC MAJESTY OR OF HIS MAJESTY'S ALLIES.

REGULATIONS will be published in due course for the proper ordering and control of the inhabitants of the districts occupied by the Troops of HIS BRITANNIC MAJESTY: AND I COMMAND ALL PERSONS well and truly TO OBEY THESE REGULATIONS AND ALL ORDERS GIVEN by me or by any person acting UNDER MY AUTHORITY.

GIVEN under my hand this first day of December, 1918, at my General Headquarters.

D. HAIG, Field-Marshal,
Commanding-in-Chief, British Armies.

An die Bevölkerung aller von den britischen Truppen besetzen Stadte und Ortschaften.

ICH WEISE DARAUF HIN, dass JEDES VORGEHEN welches das Leben BRITISCHER HEERESANGEHORIGER gefährdet oder die Operationen der BRITISCHEN TRUPPEN storen könnte, als feindselige Handlung angesehen wird. Es ist jedermanns PFLICHT, insbesondere von Staats-und stadtischen Beamten, bei der Unterdrückung irgendwelcher Verstosse gegen meine Verordnungen Beistand zu leisten.

ALLEN- EINWOHNERN DIESES ORTES WIRD DIE PERSONLICHE SICHERHEIT GARANTIERT, wenn sie sich in ergebener und friedlicher Weise verhalten. Indessen wird nachdrücklich darauf hingewiesen, dass die Nichtbefolgung dieser Verordnungen durch die Bevölkerung dieses Ortes die völkerrechtlich vorgeschriebene Strafe nach sich zieht.

DIE BEREITWILLIGKEIT, MEINEN ANORDNUNGEN FOLGE ZU LEISTEN, WIRD DIE BESTE BURGSCHAFT FUR DIE SICHERHEIT DER EINWOHNER SEIN.

ES WIRD DARAUF AUFMERKSAM GEMACHT, DASS:

1. JEDE FEINDSELIGE HANDLUNG gegen BRITISCHE HEERESANGEHORIGE, jeder Diebstahl oder Beschädigung von Gegenstanden und Materialien, die der britischen Militärbehorde gehören,
2. jede BESCHADIGUNG oder UNBRAUCHBARMACHUNG irgendwelcher Gebäude, Strassen, Eisenbahnen, Kanäle, Brucken, Telegraph-Fernsprech-und Wasserleitungen, Materialien oder wenn solche Anlagen oder Materialien durch irgendwelche Handlung gestort, unsicher gemacht oder in unbrauchbaren Zustand gesetzt werden,

zur Folge haben wird, dass die verantwortlichen Personen, sowie Versucher oder Anstifter, vor ein Kriegsgericht gestellt und, wenn sie für schuldig erklärt, mit dem TODE oder nach meinem Erachten bestraft werden.

ES WERDEN AUCH IN STRENGSTER WEISE BESTRAFT:

1. Ein jeder, der einen deutschen oder anderen dem britischen Reiche feindlichen Soldaten oder irgendjemanden der GEGEN MEINE ANORDNUNGEN VERSTOSSEN HAT, IN SCHUTZ NIMMT oder VERSTECKT, oder auf anderer Weise Hilfe leistet.
2. Ein jeder, der irgendwelchen ihm bekannten VERKEHR mit den Feinden des britischen Reiches verbirgt oder nicht anzeigt.
3. Ein jeder, der allen ihn und seine Mobilien und Immobilien betreffenden Verordnungen NICHT UNVERZUGLICH FOLGE LEISTET.
4. Ein jeder, der sich einer Handlung, ob dieselbe durch besondere Anordnung verboten ist oder nicht, schuldig macht, welche gegen die Ordnung verstösst oder die Gesundheit oder Sicherheit britischer oder verbundeter Truppen oder Staatsangehörigen gefährdet.

Es werden ausführliche BEKANNTMACHUNGEN zwecks Inordnunghaltung und Kontrollierung der Einwohner der von den britischen Truppen besetzten Gebiete zur rechten Zeit veroffentlicht werden.

DIESEN, SOWIE ALLEN ANDEREN VON MIR ODER MEINEN VERTRETERN VEROFFENTLICHTEN ANORDNUNGEN, MUSS UNBEDINGT FOLGE GELEISTET WERDEN.

GOD SAVE THE KING.

238 FRANCE December 1918 Proclamation

Peace Day.

HYDE PARK HOTEL.   Le 28 Juin, 1919.

241 BRITAIN April 1920 Disablement discharge certificate

242 BRITAIN November 1919
Magazine cover

MISSING.

ANY RETURNED PRISONER of WAR, who may have seen or heard of SECOND LIEUT. IAN GUNNIS, Grenadier Guards, reported missing near Boesinghe, July 4th, 1917, is earnestly begged to COMMUNICATE with his mother, Hon. Mrs. Gunnis, 9, Hill-street, Berkeley-square, London, W.1.

CAPTAIN T. H. HUDSON, 5th Royal Berkshires, missing Oct. 13th, 1915. INFORMATION from repatriated prisoners earnestly desired.—Rev. T. Hudson, Great Shefford Rectory, Lambourne, Berks.

INFORMATION REQUIRED.—Would the English or Irish Medical Officer who, as a prisoner of war, voluntarily attended British wounded prisoners at the German Hospital in the factory at Le Cateau between March 21st and April 10th, 1918, kindly COMMUNICATE with Mr. H. H. Bolton, Heightside, Newchurch-in-Rossendale, Lancashire?

THE charge for announcements in this column is 7s. 6d. for two lines (minimum) and 3s. 6d. for each additional line. A line comprises about seven words.

GRANDIN.—Will any officer or man returning from the Western Front (repatriated prisoner or otherwise) and has seen or heard of the "RESTING PLACE" of LIEUT. RICHARD JOHN GRANDIN, A.S.C., attached R.F.C., reported "Missing" 18th May, 1917, afterwards officially reported "Killed in action on that date," very kindly COMMUNICATE with his wife, who would be very grateful, as she has never received any information or details? He was last seen diving into two German two-seaters (whilst flying "Scout") about 8 o'clock in the morning, Arras district.—Kindly write Mrs. R. J. Grandin, 58, Anson-road, London, N.7.

MAJOR DAVIS, 1/11 London Regt., missing 15th Aug., 1915, Gallipoli, seen in a camp in Asia Minor. INFORMATION from returned prisoners gratefully received by Mrs. Davis, 39, Cavendish-road, Brondesbury, N.W.

MAJOR T. M. JAQUES and CAPTAIN ARTHUR JAQUES, West Yorks, reported missing at Loos, Sept., 1915.—Their mother, Mrs. Allan Gunn, Red Lodge, Bassett, Hants, will be grateful for any INFORMATION regarding them.

1/6 DEVONS.—R. T. VIVIAN, Captain, R.A.M.C. Reported missing March 8th, 1916, at Duraiiah Redoubt, Mesopotamia. Any INFORMATION relating to him from his brother officers or repatriated prisoners of

243 BRITAIN January 1919 News cutting (*The Times*)

244 FRANCE 1915
Diploma of Honour and Glory

PLEASE BUY THIS LEAFLET Price 1d.

and help an unemployed

Ex-Gunner A. E. MARTIN, M.M. and Bar.

(Late R.F.A., Somersets, Devons and R.E.)

It is just a simple story
  That I want to tell to you;
Yet, in spite of its simplicity,
  It is, alas, too true.

I'm but a discharged soldier,
  Who once answered duty's call
Now forgotten by my country,
  Left to wither and to fall.

When I saw that I was needed,
  I joined up so full of pride;
They said I was a hero then,
  But now I am cast aside.

Like the song called "Playthings,"
  I am one of England's toys;
Life is but a drama,
  With its sorrows and its joys.

I have tramped along the highways,
  I have searched each city through;
But good luck never comes my way
  I can find no work to do.

And this is England's gratitude,
  To the men who fought and bled;
They reward us with a medal,
  Then we're left to want for bread

So now you know my story,
  I ask you, if you can,
To try and buy this leaflet
  From an Ex-service man.

And now, ladies and gentlemen, after serving nearly four years in France, and also North Russia after the war, I am compelled to do this to get an honest living.   Hoping you will kindly buy a copy.

NO PENSION.   My Army Papers can be shown.

I WILL CALL BACK LATER.

SHOULD BE GLAD OF ANY WORK.

G.H.Q., FRANCE.
              June, 1918.

To No. 40293 Lance Bdr. A. E. MARTIN, R.F.A.
  I congratulate you on the gallant act by which you have won the Bar to the Military Medal.   (Signed) H. RAWLINSON,
              General Commanding 4th Army Corps.